C000001407

BORROWING FROM THE FUTURE

Borrowing from the Future

*A Faith-Based Approach to
Intergenerational Equity*

ANN MORISY

continuum

Published by the Continuum International Publishing Group

The Tower Building	80 Maiden Lane
11 York Road	Suite 704
London	New York
SE1 7NX	NY 10038

www.continuumbooks.com

© Ann Morisy, 2011

All rights reserved. No part of this publication may be reproduced or transmitted in any form or by any means, electronic or mechanical, including photocopying, recording or any information storage or retrieval system, without prior permission from the publishers.

First published 2011

British Library Cataloguing-in-Publication Data
A catalogue record for this book is available from the British Library.

ISBN: 978-1441-12536-1

Typeset by Fakenham Prepress Solutions, Fakenham, Norfolk NR21 8NN
Printed and bound in Great Britain

Contents

Acknowledgements

I should like to thank the following people for their help and encouragement: Margaret Kesterton, Simon Grigg, Claire Pinney and Caroline Chartres of Continuum.

I should also like to thank all those involved in supporting the work of PSALM, particularly St Pancras Church on Euston Road. PSALM's strap-line is 'Taking ageing and faith seriously', and that is the purpose of this book.

The cartoon by Mike Turner 'I ♣ grannies' is reproduced by kind permission of PRIVATE EYE magazine / Mike Turner.

The cartoon by Ron Wood is taken from 'St Gargoyle's' © Canterbury Press and used with permission.

The author is grateful to Martin Ross for permission to use his cartoon 'Have you had the batteries out of your grandad's pacemaker?' originally published in The Cartoonist.

Every effort has been made to trace copyright holders and the publishers would be pleased to correct any omissions in any subsequent edition/s of this book.

Introduction

Baby boomers are poised to take more out of the system than they have put in. This apparently lucky generation will require younger generations to dig deep to provide the resources needed as it grows older and older. This impending crisis is scrutinized in newspapers and TV documentaries. So much analysis without some action to sort things out will soon lead to the cry 'it's not fair', and the festering of resentment among those who see themselves as the disadvantaged generations. This issue of justice between the generations is part of a larger concern: how justice is to be spread out into the future as well as *here now*.

I write as a baby boomer, and on reflection it does indeed seem as if I have had an uninterrupted stream of benefits throughout my life. But maybe I and my fellows are in for a shock. Our confident expectation of financial security rolling steadily into deep old age is threatened. The collapse of banks and the ensuing unsustainable mountain of debt that nations face mean that the future is going to be tough – even for the blessed generation of baby boomers. All the components are lining up for an intense bushfire[1] as baby boomers and younger generations have to come to terms with their – oops! I mean 'our' – hampered desire to acquire and consume.

The dastardly bushfire

Bushfires or wildfires are natural phenomena, but their frequency and intensity have been increased by human activity. We know the factors that make an area prone to a bushfire so it is possible to take precautions, but the danger can never be eradicated. Some vegetation adds to the speed of the fire: low growing vegetation provides a ladder for the flames, and some trees, the eucalyptus especially, benefit from the fire, and add to the spread of the fire as their leaves contain flammable oil. This *powerful but selfish adaptation* thus ensures the germination of their seeds, and in the process, clearing the vicinity of rival species of trees. And finally, once started, a bushfire is a devil to put out. A dastardly progression indeed, except for the well-adapted eucalyptus that thrives whilst everything else is consumed.

Suddenly we have less and less confidence that progress can flow into the future and embrace future generations. Instead, the trajectory points towards life getting tougher for younger and future generations. This disadvantaging of younger age groups is a rare occurrence in the history of western societies; in fact it is a rarity in the history of humankind. The usual flow of advantage is future-directed, with a reliable expectation that upcoming generations will have an easier life, even if only marginally easier than previous generations. Disruption to this pattern might have occurred because of natural disaster, disease or warfare, but rarely because of a worrisome knot of social, economic and demographic factors such as we face today.

This complicated and tricky scenario points to increasing competition between generations. Rivalry within a population has to be addressed carefully. Tinder-dry primeval emotions are ever-present and easily aroused, and raw, primitive emotions have to be tended gently and carefully. This is why the new phenomenon of the greying of nations, and the scope for resentment by less favoured and numerically smaller, younger generations, presents such a challenge. It is uncharted territory that will require a generosity of spirit from everyone, regardless of age, if such novel terrain is to be successfully negotiated.

A scarcely veiled threat?

The most deplorable thing about the government continuing to land students with more and more debt is that they got their education free. They'll do fine for pensions, they have little debt and made a fortune in property by buying it when they were our age. What will our generation get? Ten years of paying off debts, a laughable pension that'll be worth less than we pay in and the prospect of paying extortionate rents to the very generation who lucked out. We are the jilted generation and one day we'll all realize it and do something about it.[2]

Those of us who are baby boomers have a particular challenge in relation to all this, because history could come to describe us as the generation that could never recognize when it had had enough, and devoured the future as a consequence. Or our history could tell of how we became a pivot generation that faced up to the consumption that threatens the decay of the culture and the gouging of the land and sea, by behaving generously and imaginatively.

Environmental issues and the extinction of species are close cousins of this issue of intergenerational fairness; all of them highlight how we are taking so much today that it is hazardous for the future, not just future generations but for the future of the species Homo sapiens and the future of the planet itself. It is tempting to hold the issues of environmental threats and intergenerational fairness in tandem because they are indeed closely related. However, to do this would add to the already complex task of exploring the dynamics that make for fairness – or unfairness – between the generations. So there will be few references to environmental concerns in this book, but as we consider the extent to which we are borrowing from the future, the growing rumble of concern about environmental disruption needs to be ever present.

Generalizations are as good as it gets!

Intergenerational equity, and reflecting on the needs of future unknown and unknowable generations, calls for all kinds of generalizations. So while depicting baby boomers as a generation delighting in plenty, there are many of this generation for whom life will have been significantly nasty, mean, brutish and short. And while younger age groups will indeed have to dig deep to pay for the benefits and frivolities of older generations, many will also benefit from generous inheritance and timely support from the Bank of Mum and Dad. Generalizations stretch and re-shape reality and ride roughshod over particularities. Despite these hazards, ensuring the flow of justice into the future is too important to be ducked because of the fear of cliché and generalization. So while exceptions will always be found, they should not be allowed to defuse the challenges we face.

Even talk of *generations* can be irksome. There are no clear boundaries to distinguish when one generation gives way to another; the 'markers' that separate one generation from another can at best be only impressionistic. Nevertheless, the events and conditions each of us experience, especially in our formative years, have an impact on the way we see the world and the choices we are inclined to make during our life, and this makes for something like a generational personality. And to this generalization I add a qualifier: the conditions that prevail now, and have done for the last three decades, mean that our lives have 'become increasingly non-linear, unpredictable, and unchartable.'[3] The consequence is that none of us, regardless of generation, is likely to know what to do for the best, so all generations, whether old or young, now have a common denominator: that of having to feel our way tentatively to a viable and sustainable future.

A word in the ear to Christians

In grappling with this elusive but non-negotiable issue of how to hold off our desires and desiring for the sake of the future, I want to challenge Christians to make this a priority at the heart of discipleship. However, I seek to write in a way that is suitable for those of no faith or little faith, as well as for those who are confident as Christians. This is a challenge I take on willingly, because to write for Christians, offering thoughts and ideas that only work for Christians, would be oddly perverse, when as Christians we are quick to claim the global relevance of our faith and the contribution that the Christian faith can make to a just, peaceful and sustainable future here on earth.

There are resources that the Christian tradition provides us for thinking about this very pressing and novel moral problem, not least because Christianity urges people to resist blaming and scapegoating. The reason for this is straightforward: Jesus proclaimed himself to be the final scapegoat who puts an end to making others carry the blame for our discomfort.[4] This refusal to blame is a vital attribute in the achievement of inter-generational fairness; otherwise blame will be foisted upon older generations, angry resentment fostered, and nothing achieved at all in terms of creative and sustainable responses.

When trying to puzzle out how to take account of the future as well as the *here now*, while also embracing a discipline of *no blame*, there has to be a commitment to honest thinking and a generosity of spirit. Historically such traits have not always been associated with institutional Christianity. However, the weakening of the power of the Church has brought with it a boon: when no longer pre-occupied with the trappings of power, the established church can make room for Jesus – Jesus the man, Jesus who lived over two thousand years ago and who lived in a very distinctive way. When the Church is shorn of power, it no longer needs to avert the eyes of believers from the daily, subversive performance of the man Jesus. When we look at the behaviour and teaching of Jesus we get valuable clues about how to unfurl justice, mercy and grace, both today and into the future.

A word in the ear to those with little or no faith

For those without any faith, drawing on Christian resources may present a tricky hurdle. My suggestion is that references to Jesus are viewed in the same way as references to Mahatma Gandhi might be made. Both are historic figures who taught and coached people in the ways of peace, generosity of spirit and humility, and these characteristics, along with others, we shall need to harness if we are to rise to the challenge of achieving fairness between generations both now and into the future. However, there is one aspect of Jesus which differs from Mahatma Gandhi: Jesus claims to provide an adequate response to human dastardliness – that sneaky wickedness that is corporate and individual, conscious and unconscious, seen and unseen.

There is something alluring about the word *dastardly*. I use the word dastardly instead of the much simpler word *sin*. I do this because the word sin has little resonance in a secular society, but the failure to recognize sin does not mean that it has no impact. As we puzzle how to pivot, to turn ourselves around and turn the issue of intergenerational fairness around, we are confronted by sin – dastardliness, our own, other people's and the dastardliness that runs deep and furtively through our world. Jesus provides a path through this dastardliness. For those who are Christians this way through is secured through Jesus' death and resurrection, but Christians and non-Christians alike will be interested in how, by showing us how to live, Jesus also provides a path through dastardliness.

Action as much as analysis

I endeavour to provide more than just analysis in this book. There are a growing number of analytical works on this theme; this is because understanding the issue of intergenerational fairness requires insights from disciplines such as economics, politics, demography, sociology, psychology, health care, public policy – and the list could go on. However, analysis alone is not enough. We have reached a point where the longstanding, implicit contract of support that exists between the generations, if it is to continue, needs a show of positive intent from seniors. This means we have to move beyond analysis to response. This is why I challenge my own generation to become a *pivot generation,* willing to embrace a different standard of living and to cast aside the automatic pursuit of self-interest. I also conclude that this would not be a wholly unattractive lifestyle, with rewards that are likely to outweigh the sacrifices.

The first three chapters set out the predicament: a large generation that has been lucky followed by younger generations that appear to be less lucky. To understand the predicament it is necessary to explore the exceptional dynamics that have brought us to this position. These dynamics have cultural, demographic, economic and political aspects. In the light of these exceptional dynamics, new approaches have to be pioneered, and this includes a reappraisal of theological ideas that may have particular relevance to the *zeitgeist* we have fashioned – and which in turn fashions us. This consideration of 'second-chance' theology is the subject of Chapter Four.

Intergenerational equity also needs to take account of the distinctive contributions that different age groups potentially make to the wellbeing of a society. And this raises the possibility of a remarkable twist: could it be that the increasing ageing of the population, although presenting problems, may also be the basis for an about-turn? Might the ageing of our populations provide the wherewithal to rise to the urgent challenge of honouring the future? This is the focus of Chapter Five.

Chapters Six and Seven consider the matters of retirement and inheritance. Both of these issues, in their broadest sense, are significant carriers of unfairness. In these two chapters I also begin to explore the scope for older people to act as a 'pivot' that turns the direction of advantage. Chapter Eight explores some of the everyday ways in which older people can be burdensome to younger generations, and recommends ways of avoiding such an outcome.

Chapters Nine and Ten are altogether heavier, in an emotional rather than intellectual sense. In Chapter Nine I explore narcissism and the way in which it adds to overvaluing 'today' at the expense of tomorrow. The issue of assisted dying and the difficulty of being in one's right mind in making such a decision, as well as an exploration of what makes for a good death, are considered in Chapter Ten. The final chapter, Chapter Eleven, looks at the dynamic of resentment and the habit of blaming, and also issues a challenge to my generation to join a pivotal movement.

My aim is to stimulate conversation and debate. To help this I have included some questions to stimulate discussion. These discussions may be in a specially convened group, seeking to consider the issue of intergenerational fairness, or they may just be conversation starters between people that provide a welcome change from the usual hairdresser type conversation that begin, 'Are you going away this year?'

Notes

1. I use the metaphor 'bushfire' because the phenomena we face have similar characteristics to a bushfire or wildfire.
2. By B. Morgan, BBC News Website, readers comments 1 December 2003 and cited in E. Howker and S. Malik, *Jilted Generation*, London: Icon Books, 2010 p.199
3. R. Zemke, C. Raines and B. Filipczak, *Generations at Work*, New York: Amacom, 2000 p.13
4. Jesus also demonstrated the futility of scapegoating by defying the death that was imposed by those who wanted to be rid of him. Jesus is

the scapegoat who died and conquered death and puts an end to the bloodletting that begins with blaming and ends in murderous actions. This is the case made most thoroughly by the anthropologist René Girard. This theme is explored in Chapter Eleven.

CHAPTER ONE

Uniquely favoured? Uniquely selfish? Uniquely fearful?

For Londoners one of the most celebrated possessions is the free travel pass that comes when you reach your sixties. Such liberation and such generosity: free, unrestricted travel on buses, tubes and trains across the capital. However, not everyone sees it like this. In contrast to the rejoicing of the Third-Agers, a friend's daughter of nineteen splutters with fury as she pays full fare while noting well-heeled working professionals flaunting their orange 'pensioner' pass. 'It's not fair', she protests and takes umbrage at fortunate older travellers. With such visible advantage accruing to older people, the reluctance of some younger people to offer their seat to older travellers becomes more understandable.

Even for the wealthy?

The majority of FTSE 100 chairmen are over 60, and therefore receive the £200 fuel allowance and free bus passes, or more likely the generous London Freedom pass.

Those born in 1948 will now be well-practised in the art of free travel. In fact the word 'free' is a characteristic of that post-war age group. The year 1948 has been singled out as the most fortunate year in which to have been born. So says Caroline Davies, as she lists free healthcare, free education, free love and the scope for retirement relatively free of financial worries that have accrued to the 1948ers. 'Nourished and nurtured by a "cradle-to-grave" welfare state and protected by final salary, the holy grail of pension schemes, the 1948ers would appear to have had it all.'[1] As well as financial and material security these early baby boomers have enjoyed the gifts brought by technology – before the gridlocks and malfunctions came into view. Delight came repeatedly to the 1948ers:

> The magic was that whenever us 48ers got to a certain age, the world delivered just what we were looking for. We wanted sex? Suddenly there was the Pill! We wanted to rebel, take lots of drugs and do the things our parents never did? Blow me down, along came flower power. It's as if we had ordered things from a celestial menu. No – we didn't even have to order them – they were delivered to our door.[2]

The achievement of such prodigious and long lasting pleasure-seeking suggests that the parable of the prodigal son may, over the last sixty years, have morphed into the story of prodigal mum and dad.

While I am not one of the 'have it all' 1948ers, I do have to own up to being part of the generation that Harold Macmillan suggested 'had never had it so good'. As part of the post-war baby boom (roughly those born between 1945 and 1965) I can boast of having been issued with my own ration book and I can remember the bomb sites that marked the neighbourhood. However, rather than the hardship, just like the

1948ers the story that has run through my life has been that of ever-increasing benefits and affluence. While the parents of the baby boom generation may have faced fear, deprivation and the loss of loved ones through warfare, the post-war, boom generation benefited from the war-traumatized generation's determination to make the world a better place.

They say that we resemble our times more than we resemble our parents. While we are not prisoners of the subtle and not so subtle cultural messages of our era, they trickle down with great effect and forge generational styles that earn labels such as Generation X, Y or Z (the Net generation) or simply 'The Boomers'. As a result, we all have much in common with the fellow members of our age cohort. My perception is that my age cohort was shaped by a culture characterized by optimism and a suggestion of superiority. I have a memory of my junior school, with class sizes of forty or more children, crowded into classrooms made of high, glazed brick walls. However, in each of those classrooms would be a map of the world that was mostly coloured pink – the British Empire not yet transformed into the Commonwealth. I remember my father, who like so many others of his age cohort had spent a formative part of his life fighting for his country, being keen to encourage pride in being British: 'This is the best country in the world to be born in' he would proudly insist. He also coached me to recite the features that made my home city of Liverpool one of the greatest places in the world, concluding the recitation with reference to the 'Mammoth' – the largest floating crane in the world, taken from Germany as a 'spoil of war'[3].

For those of us born after the Second World War, the baby boomers, while sugar might have been in short supply, we became the beneficiaries of a continual unfurling of welfare provision: in modest ways such as National Health orange juice, or more major breakthroughs such as polio vaccination or commitment to free education, the world became a more and more benign place for the children of those who survived World War II. Macmillan was right; no generation had had it so good. And more than this, we baby boomers absorbed the idea that such advances and benefits would flow seamlessly into the future. However, this message of optimism and pride and the sense of being part of a favoured nation at a favoured time could easily drift towards narcissism and a naïve assumption that personal wellbeing was assured. What else was one to conclude when the National Health Service had plied us with rosehip syrup and vaccinated us for diphtheria, polio and scarlet fever, and in school the morning 'playtime' for infants and juniors began with the 'gill' bottle of milk?

The state, and increasingly financially secure parents, invested in this baby boom generation in a way that no previous generation had done. As a result, the toddlers of the 50s absorbed with their mother's milk, and Cow and Gate, a sense that the world revolved around them. Not only did this generation bulge, it also had a sense of being 'special': new little princes and princesses for whom the world had waited for so long – and fought for with such passion. The ever-alert media also picked up on this idea of children being precious and privileged. I recall each Saturday spending pocket money on the 'Princess', a pretty and glittery confection that avoided describing itself as a comic for girls like 'Bunty' and 'Judy'. This junior magazine was a precursor of what was to follow. The message was beginning to flow that, rather than determination and commitment and being nice to people, and venerating the school badge,[4] image, style and fashion were now the things to aim for in life.

More than enough to go round

It might be thought that being part of a big and bulky generation, bigger than what had gone before and bigger than the following generations, would be a disadvantage. One might anticipate that, with large numbers, competition for resources would increase. The fact that this did not happen was due to the coinciding of technological and social innovation, as well as upbeat markets for goods and services. In the decade following World War II, although rationing of food and clothing was still in place, high levels of employment brought steady tax revenues to underpin and encourage new welfare benefits and entitlements. This high level of employment was due in part to post-war reconstruction, but it was also supported by the growth of manufacturing as the market for consumer goods began to develop. The combination of increasing tax revenues and the hard-won determination to make the world a better place energized social policy: opening up education, extending health care, introducing national insurance to provide support through the hazards of long-term sickness and old age, and even 'state benefit' to assist while unemployed.

Three jobs in a day

I recall an older friend of mine reminiscing about his early experience of employment. He had been 'called-up' for military service towards the end of World War II and had been sent to fight in Korea. He survived to tell the tale, but he can also tell the tale of how there were lots of good jobs in the 1950s and 60s. He tells of how he was (yet again!) late for work and was sacked. He walked along the road to another factory and presented himself to the manager who immediately set him to work. But he didn't like the job, so at lunchtime he left and walked a bit further down the road and presented himself to another employer – who immediately gave him a job, a job which suited him just fine. Not only were jobs plentiful, men's work was often financially rewarding. Unskilled and semi-skilled work was plentiful, and with strong trade unions it was relatively well paid. And it was not just jobs for men that were available; for young women especially, new 'caring' professions were emerging that offered job satisfaction, scope for promotion and pensionable service.

Although schooling was plagued by the hazard of the '11 plus', success in the exam opened up exceptional opportunities. Success at secondary level education brought the possibility of free higher education in new polytechnics and universities – all supported by a student grant. This brought about unprecedented social mobility as 'delaying gratification' (i.e. staying on at school and going to college!) brought obvious rewards as aristocracy gave way to meritocracy. Investing in education, for those of the post-war baby boom, bore evident fruits as qualifications opened doors to the new phenomenon of 'career', both for young men and young women from the Grammar schools despite having regional accents rather than 'received pronunciation'[5].

The growth of the economy in the 1950s through to the early 1970s brought, even to working-class households, the necessary disposable income to match the increasing availability of consumer goods. For those who were employed, whether in unskilled or semi-skilled jobs, the chances were that after the bills had been paid there would still be money left over, and the desires of newly affluent working-class households for a holiday abroad and a car and … house ownership became undistinguishable from the desires and expectations of middle-class households. Affluence was no longer confined to the middle class; it had become the experience and expectation of the majority. And in addition to all this, there was another advantageous dynamic, as well as a vibrant job market, that would also serve to blur the boundaries between the social classes: it was the housing market.

Investing in your own house was, without question, the thing to do. The returns on the investment in property were indisputable, and Building Societies were happy to aid and abet, as wages became salaries and the ideal of a property-owning democracy was the ultimate achievement for the 'You have never had it so good' generation. Mortgages and bijou living became the symbols of freedom and one of the 'soft power' weapons of the Cold War, aimed at delivering a knock-out blow to communist-styled ideologies fostered by the USSR, the feared opponent behind an 'iron curtain'.

Forgive my reminiscing, but I, like others, find it hard to resist the property owning riff – that compulsive beat that runs through the lives of baby boomers. I think I was 24, a single woman, when I bought my first house. I mustered £400 as five per cent deposit on a modest terraced house. Ten years later I sold it for £35,000. On the back of this effortless largess I took myself to London and risked what then seemed like a gargantuan mortgage, only to be again rewarded for that risky wager. This feel-good factor of an increasingly valuable house has buoyed the baby boomer generation in a way that was unknown in the past, and is likely to be unknown in the future. (See box 'The crowning advantage' for a blow by blow account of how this came about).

The crowning advantage: Owning your own house

The advantage that accrues from house ownership is a complex generational phenomenon. It is based on the distinctive economic and political circumstances through which the baby boom generation has lived. For example, house owners (including many of those with mortgages) benefit from inflation. The impact of inflation in the 1970s and 80s brought a rise in earnings, thus making the price paid for a house an ever-lessening proportion of one's income. And note: the fact that wages kept in step or even ahead of inflation was a product of the strength of trade union power at that time.

In addition to the impact of inflation, legislation significantly benefited home owners. For most of the 1960s and 70s there were significant tax advantages and financial incentives available to owner-occupiers, making home ownership by far the best deal for ordinary people. And the converse of this: the fact that mortgage payments could be offset against tax significantly disadvantaged those who continued to rent their homes.

Today, the advantage that exists for house owners is due to the changing shape of households. The fact that there are now more single-person households than ever before has added to the competition for property, and this has continued to drive up prices.

These advantages for a generation of house owners understandably get judged as unfair, because these gains in wealth have not come from personal effort or prudent decisions made during one's life. The advantages are due to a particular, and probably unrepeatable, pattern of political and economic circumstances. Most people refer to this as luck.

Those who, like myself, were born in the 1950s, as well as being the generation that has become ensconced in high-value property, have also traversed the globe in the pursuit of pleasure. We have consumed the resources of the globe to fill our houses with possessions and trinkets, as well as discovering the convenience of disposability. All this, as well as benefiting from exponential improvements in health care and associated longevity. And now, in the sprint to retirement, there is the anticipation of financial security for a long old age...

Yikes! A hiccup!

Abruptly, the best laid plans have been up-ended and expectations are to be disappointed. We know that financial institutions have gone into melt down and few dare to speak honestly of the extent of the disarray that has followed. We have been confronted with how, in a globalized, market economy, everything is connected, and that includes our pensions. A frisson of anxiety has run through once confident sovereign states as they watch their neighbours being assaulted by market speculation and jittery markets.

Moody's Corporation and Standard and Poor's are the major global ratings agencies. They assess the credit-worthiness not just of commercial companies, but also of nations. This gives immense power as these ratings provide guidance to investors. The highest rating: AAA is prized by governments and commercial companies because a lower rating prompts the lender to charge a higher interest rate.

While some would dispute the accuracy and even the integrity[6] of these companies, the analysis they offer of the world's major market economies is stark. They do not mince their words, warning that austerity measures must be implemented if nations are to continue to receive the highest credit ratings and thus be in a position to attract potential investors, especially pension funds. Moody's have cautioned that 'Growth alone will not resolve an increasingly complicated debt equation. Preserving debt affordability at levels consistent with AAA ratings will invariably require fiscal adjustments of a magnitude that, in some cases, will test social cohesion.'[7] This code is easy to crack: in trying to pay back what they owe, or just keeping debt in check, many western nations will have to cut back on public services and benefits to such an extent that it may cause unrest in the population. This is something which we all know about first hand.

It is not just economic think tanks and ratings agencies that sense fraughtness in the future. A poll across western nations revealed that 'A solid majority of people in the major western democracies expect a rise in political extremism in their countries as a result of the economic crisis.' Of those surveyed, 53 per cent in Italy and the United States said they expected extremism is 'certain to happen' or 'probable' in the next three years. This percentage increases to 65 per cent in Britain and Germany, and is at 60 per cent in France and Spain.[8] When 'political extremism' is mentioned the quick assumption is that this means racial tension, as extremists seek to reclaim a country for the longstanding population. However, the riots in France over the raising of the retirement age in October 2010 highlighted how extremism can focus on generational issues. Young French students were quick to distinguish themselves from other, older demonstrators: students were on the streets because their futures were in jeopardy because of greedy baby boomers.

For those who have grown up with the idea that the future is controllable, these heavy clouds on the horizon are a shock. And it is likely that it is the *non-poor* who have been dispro-portionately wobbled, because poor people are already aware of how protection from the hazards of life is flimsy, and that the future has always been more likely to be laden with threat than opportunity. Even though history shows how, in every economic downturn or depression, the poor are always hit disproportionately hard, it is those who had expectations of prosperity, regardless of how modest, who are likely to feel most aggrieved as bit by bit they / we (delete as appropriate) realize how their / our savings in pension funds and endowment policies fail to return the dividend they / we had expected. We have casually skimmed the standard warning on investment applications, including pension funds, that 'you should not base decisions on past performance. Prices may fluctuate and you may not get back your original investment'. However, financially blessed baby boomers had no experience of falling or failing performance so why worry? We have suddenly learnt that the world of finance is heartless and capricious territory.

'Millions Heading for an Impoverished Future'

'The figures demonstrate that, put simply, people are not investing anywhere near enough for their retirement years,' said Philip Brown, Partnership's Head of Retirement Products... 'Our figures show that most average men and women retiring in the UK today can look forward to a State pension of under £6,000 per year, plus a private pension of around £2,000 a year... Today's average wage for men and women is hovering around £26,000, so in other words they will be obliged to live on a reduction in income of up to 70% when they stop work' warned Brown.

The situation will deteriorate further unless more people make the appropriate savings and annuity choices open to them: the number of 65-year-olds in the UK is set to increase from 9.9 million now to 15.5 million by 2030.'[9]

This sudden spectre of having to manage on meagre resources will be a severe test for those of us who have led comfortable lives. Having drifted into the assumption that wellbeing comes from buying things and that pleasure is a product that is bought, we face an extraordinary challenge. Even those who claim to have seen through the racket of materialism and the market still face the challenge of austerity. For the untested generation of non-poor baby boomers, this change in the economic climate not just shocks, but forces us into the uncharted terrain of uncertainty, no longer knowing what to do for the best, and facing the challenge of achieving a previously unknown degree of resilience.

This analysis suggests that it is the 'non-poor' who are likely to feel most betrayed as we face up to major re-adjustments in lifestyle; it is the non-poor who have invested most determinedly in a story that promised to have a happy ending. Whilst we may not be rich, we may be comfortably off in a middling sort of way and it is hard to avoid a sense of betrayal when suddenly confronted with the prospect of living for decades on puny private pensions. This new reality for baby boomers has scarcely penetrated our awareness, having for the whole of our working lives cocooned ourselves with the anticipation of a financially secure and long retirement. For those who consider themselves to have played by the rules and acted responsibly, it is likely that betrayal combines with anger. More serious still, anger may mask fear, and fear is an intense and destabilizing emotion. Jacques Ellul suggests that fear 'dictates two modes of behaviour: violence and rigidity'.[10]

Fear begets fear[11]

In Luke chapter 8 there is the story of the deranged and much-feared man who inhabited the graveyard in Gerasa. The man called himself 'Legion'. Local people were so frightened of Legion they used chains to restrain him, but he broke free even from these. But Legion is not just frightening with his raging and nakedness; he, too, is afraid. He is frightened of Jesus. He cries out to Jesus 'I beg you do not torment me'.

Fear begets fear: Legion is a frightened man and he is frightening to his neighbours, and this fear leads them to treat him in an inhumane way by trying to chain him up. Legion's fear leads him to live in a graveyard, naked and raving.

Fear is contagious and it diminishes everyone's humanity. Fear often motivates evil and destructive behaviour because when we are fearful, the temptation is to seek out and destroy what is perceived to be the cause of the fear. Fear can bring cheap solidarity as we gang up against those who are 'the problem'. And this cheap solidarity blinds us from seeing things afresh.

Jesus brought peace to the man who called himself Legion.

The story continues: When those from the vicinity came to the graveyard to see what was going on, they found Legion, dressed and in his right mind 'sitting at Jesus' feet'... 'and *they* were afraid'.

Fear can be so intense and extensive that it becomes habitual. The Gospels tell us how the people of Gerasa told Jesus to go, to leave their region because they were so overcome with fear, despite the fact that his only action was to bring peace to the deeply troubled man who lurked in the graveyard.

It is possible to be trapped in one's fear, stuck as an individual, as a neighbourhood or town or city – and maybe stuck as a generation.

In such a troubled context, there is another feature of the baby boom generation that has to be acknowledged: we baby boomers have been the protesting generation: CND, Pride,

Greenham Common, Jubilee 2000, all relied on the baby boomer generation for their momentum. Although the roots of one's hair may be grey, those of us in our fifties and sixties know what it is like to respond to suddenly imposed grievances,[12] and the thrill of solidarity that comes from this is held together by a mixture of outrage and moral indignation. So if, as in France, Greece and Spain, people take to the streets to protest about cuts and unfairness, what are the likely slogans on the banners carried by the radicalized baby boomers? Who and what are we against? Who is to be accused and made to carry the can? And most importantly, how do we balance our interest in a secure old age with the interests of younger generations that are already being squeezed? We risk an intellectual failure as well as a moral one if we allow self-interest to be the only motivation that takes us onto the streets.

This mix of a 'future gone bad', and an older generation that knows how to take its protest to the street, presents a unique challenge. How do we older people express indignation? How do we come together to try to make a better future? This challenge has a paradox at its heart, because if we baby boomers are to cry 'It's not fair', then we are two-faced and deceitful, because we are the generation that in comparison with others has been treated exceptionally fairly and has been exceptionally lucky. And yet... there does indeed appear to have been malfeasance, so do we walk away accepting that nothing can be done and our luck has run out? What are the justifiable moral categories which we can organize around? And then the question is how to express indignation in a way that does not bring havoc to an already creaking civil society?

As a radicalized generation we baby boomers know that protest is only worthwhile if the focus is on issues beyond our own interests. We know that if solidarity is to be achieved it needs a bold and broad moral foundation. So what do we do with our righteous indignation at having lost the prospect of a financially comfortable old age? Do we fight for our rights or do we stretch to achieve a wider moral concern: that of how the future can be factored in to the decisions being made today? This objective is understandably paramount for younger generations, but for older people it is more morally challenging. These are issues for everyone. However, older people, and Christians in particular, will want to reflect on how to respond to our new prospects.

Notes

1. Caroline Davies 'We should be so lucky. The 1948ers who had it all: sex, drugs, music and a pension', the *Guardian* 7 November 2009.
2. Ibid.
3. Following a thread on www.shipsnostalgia.com an urban myth of my childhood has been shattered: *Mammoth* was built by A. F. Smulders in Schiedam, Holland, originally for the Russian Tsarist Government, but the 1917 Revolution caused the sale to fail and she was sold to the Mersey Docks and Harbour Board and arrived in Liverpool in September 1920.
4. Yes, Bunty or maybe Judy invited its readers to send in a school badge for inclusion in the deck of school badges they produced each week alongside 'The Four Marys' and 'Margi the Swimming Marvel'.
5. Received Pronunciation is the term used to describe the 'cut glass' accent that was *de rigeur* on the BBC or if one had professional standing.
6. See for example A. Klein, 'Credit Raters' Power Leads to Abuses, Some Borrowers Say' *Washington Post*, November 24, 2004, and K. G. Hall, 'How Moody's sold its ratings – and sold out investors', *McClatchy Newspapers*, 18 October 2009'.
7. A. Evans-Pritchard, 'Moody's fears social unrest as AAA states implement austerity plans', the *Telegraph*, 15 March 2010.
8. J. C. Freed, 'Economic Crisis Raises Fears of Extremism in Western Countries', the *New York Times*: 6 May 2009.

9. 'Millions heading for an impoverished future,' *Mature Times*, 11 June 2010.

10. J. Ellul, (1980) *Living Faith: Belief and Doubt in a Perilous World*, trans. Peter Heinegg, New York: Harper and Row p.109.

11. These thoughts about 'Legion' are based on a sermon preached by the Rev'd Mandy Hodgson at St Leonard's Church, Streatham on 20 June 2010.

12. 'Suddenly imposed grievances' is a phrase regularly used by Edward J. Walsh in his studies of protest movements.

CHAPTER TWO

What's the score?

In the United Kingdom, the number of people over the age of 65 is expected to rise from 16 per cent in 2008 to 23 per cent by 2033. The fastest-growing age group during this period will be those over the age of 85, who are expected to double in number and account for almost five per cent of the population by 2033.[1] With statistics such as these we would do well to heed the advice given by Carl Djerassi,[2] the man who formulated the contraceptive pill. He suggests that rather than the categories of the 'developed' and 'undeveloped' world, the real division is between the geriatric and the paediatric world. The defining characteristic of the social environment of Western 'developed' nations has become that of old age, and in this experience we depart from the whole history of humankind.

It is estimated that human history covers 500 generations[3] but only in the last two generations have we had to negotiate the extensive and unremitting ageing of populations. With extraordinary rapidity we have a new demographic landscape that makes old age 'the essential, archetypal characteristic of the modern condition.'[4] It is now common, in mostly western nations, for retired people to make up a quarter of the population and for the life expectancy of women to extend easily beyond 85 years. However, this greying of the nations is due to more than just increased longevity. It is also due to a fall in the number of babies being born, and in many nations this drop has been so severe and longstanding that the population is declining. So there are two aspects to keep in mind when trying to make sense of this abrupt development: increased longevity and falling birth rates.

The novelty of this scenario cannot be overestimated; it is new to the species. No wonder governments are bemused and hesitant about how to respond. A brief summary of how the numbers add up shows the extent of this taxing development:

- Between 1950 and 2010, the world's population more than doubled in size, to 6.8 billion. During this period, the median age of the world's population rose by just three years (to 26 years).
- It is estimated that between 2010 and 2050, the world's population will rise to 8.9 billion; however the median age of the world's population will increase by 11 years (to 37 years).

We are familiar with poor nations having rapidly increasing populations with lots of youngsters. What is less acknowledged is that richer nations tend to have lots of oldsters and *shrinking* populations.[5] Paul Hodge provides some examples:

'It is predicted that the populations of 43 countries, mainly in Europe, will be lower in 2050 than they are today. Throughout the developed world, populations will be greying as the age balance tilts towards the elderly. In the European Union, for example, the elderly dependency ratio (i.e. people aged 65 or more compared with those aged 15–64) will increase from one-in-four to one-in-two. In several countries, including Japan, Italy and Singapore, the median age will rise to over 50 by 2050.'[6]

The Demographic Transition Model

Warren Thompson, an American demographer, devised the 'Demographic Transition Model' to account for the link between affluence and smaller family size. Writing in 1929[7], Thompson researched the pattern of population growth that occurred as industrialization took hold. Prior to industrial development, the rates of births and deaths were roughly in balance. However, as people began to live closer to each other in the industrial towns, the pressure for public health improvements grew, particularly in relation to sanitation, and as the improvements gained momentum the death rate began to fall, especially for children. This meant that more children survived into adulthood and in turn had children of their own.

The first stage of the demographic transition was a fall in death rates and the second stage was characterized by a rapid increase in population, as those who now survived lived long enough to have children.

The third stage in the evolution of a nation's population Thompson referred to as the 'mature industrial' stage, characterized by a fall in the birth rate. This reduction in the number of children is linked with a fall in the value of children's work, and an increase in the status of women, combined with access to contraception. As a result of this fall in the birth rate, population growth begins to level off, and the fourth stage is achieved as population stability is re-established at replacement level i.e. the rate of births and deaths roughly balancing each other.[8]

Demographers and economists have identified the possibility of a beneficial 'demographic window' which can bring a 'demographic dividend'. This occurs when the proportion of dependent youngsters is low compared with the number of working people in the population, and this provides the ingredients for economic growth. It is this 'demographic window of opportunity' that, according to a number of commentators,[9] has played an important part in the high output per capita of the East Asian Tiger economies and the economic boom experienced in Ireland in the 1990s. This window of opportunity or demographic 'bonus' can last for up to forty years, as long as employment is available for the high number of working-age people.[10] In the United Kingdom this window was estimated to have run from 1950 to 1975,[11] almost precisely when the baby boom generation began to make its way in the world. No wonder Harold Macmillan was able to boast that 'Britain had never had it so good'.

This window of opportunity slides shut when the proportionately large workforce grows old and retires and is replaced by the smaller number of young workers. As the workforce shrinks, the dependency ratio begins to rise as the larger, older population becomes dependent. This is the situation in which many advanced nations now find themselves. However, there has been a demographic phenomenon that was not predicted: the extent to which the fertility rate has fallen *below* replacement level.[12] This unexpected occurrence has taken place in most of the so-called 'advanced' nations. For example, in most European nations birth rates have fallen below replacement level and have only been spared population shrinkage by the desire of people, usually of child-bearing age, from poor parts of the world, to move to the wealthy West – and have children.

Explaining the pig in the python

War brings a great interruption to the demographic pattern of nations. The death rate shoots up and the birth rate falls in the face of fear and disruption. However, when the war ceases, the birth rate often climbs, as it did after the Second World War in Britain, Europe, the USA and Japan. What was remarkable was how this increase in the birth rate continued for almost twenty years into the early 1960s.[13] This sudden and persistent increase in births has been described rather crudely as 'the pig in the python'.[14] The post-war boom in births has resulted in an age cohort bigger than those ahead of it (the low fertility of the 1930s) and bigger than the cohort that followed through the late sixties and subsequently. The 'pig in the python' analogy, although somewhat vulgar, is perhaps appropriate, because it carries a suggestion of gorging and even greed, and if one dare risk anthropomorphizing a python, the potential for indigestion. Not only were births high, but the story of this booming generation will be forever associated with gorging and self-indulgence and, as we are discovering, a source of discomfort for younger generations.

The surge in births after the disruption of the Second World War is explained by the economic boom prompted by reconstruction across Europe, leading to high employment rates for men, combined with the closing off of employment opportunities for women – especially younger women. This happened because of the precedence given by employers to all the demobbed men. In this scenario, 'Young women, confronted with a lack of work opportunities – but an abundance of prosperous young men – getting married early and having a large family was a natural choice.'[15] Add to this the 'compression' of births due to the avoidance of getting pregnant in the midst of wartime distress, and the birth rate starts to rise significantly. Government policies also played a part, with extra pay going to soldiers with children and more and more nurseries being provided. All this, combined with the determined optimism that the world could become a better place, provided an ideal environment to pursue the idealized vision of happy families. As a result, fertility levels in Britain rose to 2.8 children per woman of child-bearing age, a level comfortably above the estimated replacement level of 2.15.

After the boom – the empty womb

Fred Pearce uses the term 'lowest-low fertility' to describe the levels of fertility now being experienced in many European nations. He uses this extreme descriptor because if such low fertility continues, even for just a decade longer, parts of Europe will experience serious depopulation. He notes:

'German, Austrian, Russian, Swiss, Spanish and Greek women in 2008 managed on average just 1.4 children each, Italians 1.3, and Czechs, Poles, Bosnians, Ukrainians and Belarusians 1.2.[16] Thirty years ago, 23 European countries had fertility above replacement levels; now none does.[17] Only France, Iceland, Albania, Britain and Ireland are anywhere near.'[18]

Pearce suggests that once a country has very low fertility for a generation, this produces a downward momentum, as the next generation has fewer potential mothers than the one before it, and there is every chance that societies will get out of the habit of having children.

Where have all the youngsters gone?

In Britain over the next 30 years, our population will age significantly. However, the main reason for this is the decline in the fertility rate. For the 20 years between 1971 and 1991, the number of youngsters under 15 decreased by about 2.6 million. Over that same 20 year period the number of people aged over 65 increased by only 1.5 million. As a result, the average age of the British population rose almost twice as much because of the fewer young people rather than because of there being more elderly people. This combination of relatively high fertility in the early 1950s and into the 1960s, only to be followed by a long period of low fertility, has produced a bulge generation that will reach retirement age from the year 2010 onwards.[19]

For women throughout Europe *not* having children has now become a socially acceptable lifestyle option. The focus on the greying of the nations easily masks this extraordinary demographic development. This contributes to the increasingly troubling dependency ratio as the generation earning and paying taxes gets smaller and smaller, in comparison with those anticipating support from services paid for by taxation. Data from the USA highlights the intensity of this issue: in 1945, the year the baby boom began, each retired person in the US was supported by 4.6 workers. Today the figure is three workers, and will fall to just two when the baby boomers start to draw their pensions.

Figures such as these are fearsome. However, there are factors that rarely get mentioned which offset the threat carried by these raw statistics:

- Although there will be a large number of older people who may potentially be dependent on few people of working age, there are likely to be fewer dependent children.
- There will be a continued increase in the economic significance of women in the workforce.
- The number of days lost through sickness and industrial disputes have the potential to remain low and even fall further.
- Medical treatment and care will continue to ensure that older people retain their capacities, so their competence and availability for work will be on hand for longer.
- Social innovation based on ingenuity and good institutions – a dynamic that has brought us from the Stone Age – will invent new patterns of social relationships that compensate for the impending 'burden' of frail older people.

You can decide for yourself to what extent you are convinced by such mitigating factors.

As well as honest and imaginative thinking, in negotiating the future we shall require extraordinary generosity of spirit. The future of most developed nations will rely on the productivity of those from the so called 'underdeveloped' nations. You could say that this has always been the case. However, the productivity of the least established in our land, and in mainland Europe, will matter more than ever into the future. It will be those who have immigrated into Britain, especially women, who will provide the care we need as we anticipate the journey into 'deep' old age. The productivity of those who have travelled to get themselves established in Britain is also important in another sense, for this is the group that is producing the children that will grow up to pay the taxes that support me and my fellow-baby boomers into our dotage.

Social cohesion always matters, but it matters even more into the future.

A growing population in England and Wales

According to the Office for National Statistics, the number of babies born in England and Wales has reached the highest level for more than 16 years. There were 691,013 births in 2007, a three per cent rise over the year before, and the highest level since 1991.

The fertility rates among women over 40 also went up by six per cent in 2007 and have doubled in the 15 years since 1992. Women over 40 gave birth to 25,350 babies in 2007, nearly double the 12,914 babies born to over 40s in 1997.

Overall, in England and Wales, based on figures for 2007 each woman is now likely to have 1.91 babies in her life, the highest fertility rate since 1973. The highest birth rates were in the West Midlands, where the average for each woman is 2.04 children.

More than one in five births were to women who were born overseas, the Office for National Statistics said.

And what the media said:

'How media is distorting the facts about birth rates and immigration' observes Siân Ruddick in relation to the stir caused by new population statistics in the press. She writes 'The data, released by the Office of National Statistics, show that the birth rate in Britain has risen over the past year, taking the population over 61 million. That's not so shocking, you might think. But the right-wing press had a field day as it emerged that 24 per cent of the babies born in 2008 were born to 'foreign' mothers – that is, mothers of a nationality other than British. The papers that day were seemingly competing to see who could be the most offensive. "Scroungers soaking up our services", screamed the Daily Express. "Immigrant baby boom", cried the Mail.'[20]

Perhaps the worst case scenario is that society so fragments that a culture of 'everyone for themselves from birth to death' prevails. The consequence of this will be that the tiny capillaries of state social provision, and the intricate inter-relationships which nourish this provision, begin to wither. While social innovation can invent other means of providing care for elders, such invention would find it difficult to withstand active resentment between the generations, and the media may find it difficult to resist the temptation to whip up and feed such resentment. Just the routine marketing by advertisers will be sufficient to implant a feeling of resentment among younger people, as more and more advertising focuses on stairlifts and bath aids and luxury cruises. Furthermore, the scope for YouTube, Facebook and Twitter to humiliate and undermine old people is already upon us. Social innovation, critical thinking and generosity of spirit are needed now if we are to avoid getting caught up in a pernicious cycle.

Notes

1. Department for Business, Innovation and Skills, *Is business ready for an ageing nation?* March 2101 p.9.
2. Carl Djerassi was born in Vienna, but has lived mostly in the USA. He is a chemist best known for his work on the development of the contraceptive pill, and is also a novelist and playwright. Djerassi expresses this idea in an interview with Martin Ince which is included in S. Griffiths (ed.) (1999) *Predictions*, Oxford: Oxford University Press p.79.
3. A generation is roughly twenty-five to twenty-seven years, and is based on the time between a mother giving birth to her first child and her daughter giving birth to her first child.
4. J. Vincent (2003) *Old Age*, London: Routledge p.1.
5. There are exceptions: For example, for the last 15 years, the Russian population has shrunk by about 0.5 per cent per year. This was due to falling birth rates and rising death rates likely to have been triggered

by the disruption associated with the dismantling of the Soviet Union. In 2009 the Russian population increased by 0.01 per cent, bringing the population of Russia close to 142 million people, having been 148 million in 1991.

6. Paul Hodge of the Global Generations Policy Initiative, in his introduction to the World Economic Forum (Davros), January 2006 'The Economic Implications of Ageing'.

7. See W. S. Thompson (1929) 'Population', *American Journal of Sociology* 34(6): 959–975.

8. The model of demographic transition that was proposed by Thompson usually gets applied to industrialized nations where life expectancy has become long and family size small. However, African nations have also faced a demographic transition, and it is a transition that has even more intensity. For much of sub-Saharan Africa the challenge is how to support elders who are caring for orphans of the HIV pandemic. In countries such as China, Kenya or Mexico the ageing of the population presents a different batch of socio-economic and even moral issues. China, the nation with the largest population in the world, faces a great shortage of 'caregivers' as family size has fallen rapidly due to its 'one child' policy and because older people have remained in rural areas, while young adults have tended to move to the cities; These two factors make it difficult to ensure formal and informal care for elders. For countries such as Kenya, Mexico and Poland, there is likewise a problem of older people being left behind. In these instances the impact of smaller family size has been exacerbated by the move of offspring not just from rural to urban areas, but to other parts of the world as the surge of globalization gains momentum.

9. See D. E. Bloom and J. G. Williamson (1998) 'Demographic Transitions and Economic Miracles in Emerging Asia', *World Bank Economic Review*, 12: 419 – 455.

10. 'This window of opportunity in a nation's population evolution has been defined by the United Nations Commission on Population and Development as the period when the proportion of children and young people under 15 years falls below 30 per cent, and the proportion of people 65 years and older is below 15 per cent. In theory such a demographic 'bonus' can last for as long as forty years dependent on the ability of the economy to provide employment for the high number of working-age people'. D. E. Bloom, D. Canning and J. Savilla (2003) 'The Demographic Dividend: A New Perspective on the Economic

Consequences of Population Change', *Population Matters Monograph* MR–1274, RAND, Santa Monica.

11. Other estimates of 'demographic windows of opportunity' made by the United Nations include China: 1990–2025; India 2010–2045; USA 1970–2010; Japan 1965–1995, Eritrea 2045–2080; Uganda and the Yemen: 2060–2090. See the report *World Population to 2300* by the Department of Economics and Social Affairs Population Division (2004); United Nations, New York

12. In developed or advanced nations replacement fertility is estimated as 2.1 children over a woman's lifetime. Globally the rate is estimated as 2.33 children per woman. For the period 2005–2010 the number of children per woman averaged 2.55.

13. In Britain, unlike the USA, there were two peaks, in 1947 and again in 1964 and 1965.

14. L. Jones (1980) *Great Expectations: America and the Baby Boom Generation*, New York: Coward, McCann and Geoghegan.

15. M. Doepke, M. Hazan and Y. D. Moaz (September 2008) 'More babies for Europe: Learning from the Post-War Baby Boom' in *Vox* www.voxeu.org.

16. The shrinking of populations of Eastern European nations is not just brought about by low fertility rates but also because of increasing death rates, especially among men.

17. This loss of population across Europe has other impacts. In addition to the 'dependency ratio' it will lead to morale-sapping 'perforated' cities and depopulated villages.

18. F. Pearce (2010) *Peoplequake,* London: Eden Project Books p.117.

19. Based on the work of P. Mullan (2000) *The Imaginary Time bomb: Why an ageing population is not a social problem.* London: I. B. Taurus, p.61.

20. S. Ruddock 'How media is distorting the facts about birth rates and immigration' in *Socialist Worker Online*, Issue 2168, 12 Sept 2009. http://www.socialistworker.co.uk/art.php?id=18938

CHAPTER THREE

Borrowing from the future

As a baby boomer I am now used to the accusations of self-indulgence and unrestrained pleasure seeking that get laid at the door of my generation. In the face of the undoubted benefits that have come our way, younger generations can indeed find much to complain about. Try this one for size:

'Not content with saddling us twentysomethings with mountains of public debt, the over 40s have started pinching our boyfriends too. There will be slim pickings left on the dating scene after ... the so-called 'cougars'[1] have had their fill. In fact, the middle-aged are stealing our entire lifestyle. We keep hearing how '50 is the new 25'. What no-one has noticed is that 25 is the new 70. Through little choice of our own, the under 30s are turning into a generation of Saffys. We look on some of our Ab Fabesque seniors falling out of nightclubs and jetting off for some 'time out' to return, no doubt, with bleached locks and those silly bead necklaces from 'a little market in Phuket.'[2]

Certainly the baby boom generation appears to have received the 'first fruits' of the modern world. In contrast, for younger generations, although well off compared with 99 per cent of people in the world's history and 90 per cent of the world today, the joys of life seem shopsoiled and stale. Appetite for life gets allied with older people, while the middle aged seem trapped in aspirations that lack lustre, or are spoiled by anxiety. This counters traditional expectations where youngsters are expected to be exuberant and venturesome, and the working householder in the ascendant and at the peak of their powers. Perhaps the looming burdens of the future weigh heavily on those who will inherit a world distressed by the thoughtless borrowing from the future by previous generations?

Whatever the cause, the outcome is clear. Our anticipation of a secure and comfortable future, regardless of what age we are, suddenly seems unaffordable. Future working generations, in addition to carrying the taxation demand associated with a growing number of older people blessed by ever increasing longevity, also have to meet the debt burden of billions paid to secure the banking system. The burden is immense, and younger generations will have to shoulder these costs. There is no ducking the evident unfairness in all this, and there is no guarantee that this unfairness will not be added to in the future.

There is no way of minimizing the reality that the future prospects of younger and upcoming generations will be more bleak than was ever anticipated by their parent generation when they were at the same stage in their lifespan. And the worry is that this differential will strain or even lead to the breaking of the contract between the generations. Vern Bengtson describes this situation as a 'cultural watershed concerning the implicit understanding of rights and obligations between age groups and generations in human societies.'[3] The watershed that Bengtson is referring to has two aspects:

- The recognition that the social provision and pension rights enjoyed by older generations are only possible by borrowing from the future, and that such borrowing against future wealth has been, *until now*, an unquestioned habit of modern states.
- Previous population booms were measured in terms of babies being born; this population boom is measured in terms of the growing number of old and very old people. When this combines with ever increasing medical expertise, then the cost of sustaining population growth among those in the final stage of the lifespan has become vastly more expensive.

The contract between the generations presents a very specific challenge that has always been with us, but it has come to the forefront as we recognize how it will play out in our own lifetime, or in the lifetime of our children and grandchildren. It is dawning on us that the challenge is how to honour our 'vertical obligations' to future generations in addition to the 'horizontal obligations' to those 'here now', i.e. the horizontal obligations with which we are much more familiar. David Willetts puts it 'We need to do much better at weighing the claims of the Nows versus the Laters.'[4] This is the same challenge that we face in relation to environmental degradation, where likewise we have to find ways of kindling commitment to this unseen and easily neglected vertical obligation. As well as challenging us individually, this need to attend to the future confronts our democratic processes, because democracy is in the hands of the 'here nows' and the generations to come have no voice other than that which can be expressed through our conscience.

It's not fair ... the generosity at the heart of the Kingdom of God

Jesus gives us a parable to show the nature of the Kingdom of God. The way things work in the Kingdom of God do not accord with our established sense of fairness.

Jesus describes how, early in the morning, the owner of a vineyard went and hired men to work in his vineyard. Later in the day he hired more people to work in his vineyard, and likewise he went to the market place two more times during the same day to hire more labourers. The vineyard owner chose to pay those whom he hired last the same amount as he had agreed to pay those who had worked for him all day.

Those who had worked all day were angry at this apparent unfairness. 'They began to grumble against the landowner. "These men who were hired last worked only one hour," they said, "and you have made them equal to us who have borne the burden of the work and the heat of the day." '[5]

This parable suggests that our commitment to 'fairness' can prompt us to resent generosity to the extent of wishing it away. It would seem we have to practise being comfortable with God's economy of generosity more than our culture currently inclines us to be.

Demography trumps democracy

There is an essential weakness at the heart of democracy: democracy is subject to the will of the majority, but can only be an integrative force in a society if those most in need are the most numeric – and likely to vote. In relation to intergenerational fairness, and assuming the casting of a vote is predominantly an expression of self-interest, then the larger number of older people compared to younger people in our population easily translates into political priorities that favour older people. Older people now form a majority group within most western democracies, so therefore it is unlikely any political party can achieve power without appealing to this group. This structural weakness at the heart of our democratic process seems destined to benefit the older at the expense of the younger. In Britain the statistics make this clear:

- The proportion of over 65s living in low-income households fell from 28 per cent in 1994/95 to 18 per cent in 2007/08 i.e. a reduction of ten per cent.
- The proportion of children living in low-income households fell from 33 per cent in 1994/5 to 31 per cent in 2007/08 i.e. a reduction of two per cent.
- The proportion of working-age adults with dependent children living on low income was 26 per cent in 1994/5 and remained at 26 per cent in 2007/08 i.e. no change.

Figures such as these[6] indicate that in Britain those over 65 (pensioners) are significantly less likely to be living in low-income households than non-pensioners. The capacity for government policy to alleviate poverty in relation to older people has proved far more effective than it has in relation to younger households. There may be complex reasons for this, but such statististical revelations easily fire resentment and strain the contract between the generations, as well as putting a question mark over the inherent integrity of our democratic process.

This is quite a predicament. The democratic process that we have relied upon to distribute at least a modicum of justice between the 'haves' and the 'have nots' is unlikely to bring fairness between the generations. So far no-one on the political stage has countenanced a way of holding off the growth in entitlements for elders, even when implementing substantial budget cuts, and this may be due to the two-fold brace that restrains politicians from tampering with the benefits received by older people: the issue of the proportion of older voters in the population, and the reality that policies that affect older people are not just policies 'for them'; they become policies 'for us', because all of us are potential beneficiaries of the benefits that accrue to older people. This balance of advantage towards older people leads Thomson to observe scathingly that there are two welfare systems in place, and that this has been the case for many decades:

'People of the "welfare generation",[7] have always been net beneficiaries of the welfare state, and wish to remain so into their very comfortable retirement, despite enjoying a higher income, more assets and greater economic security than many younger households... Despite a clear rise since the mid–1970s in the number of young adults with dependent children living at or below the poverty line, the real value of welfare benefits and tax concessions to this age group has fallen, whereas the increasingly asset-rich elderly have maintained or improved the value of their state pension entitlements.'[8]

'In effect, at the same time (*as there is*) a modern welfare state offering a wide range of benefits through all of one's life phases for the initiators of the welfare state, there is a minimal, means-testing welfare state of the old safety-net type for their successors.'[9]

David Thomson was an early commentator on the growing unfairness between the generations, alerting policy makers to the long term unaffordability of the entitlements that were being allocated during times of economic plenty, and highlighting the implications of unconsidered borrowing from the future. Basically, the way in which pensions are paid for is not from a pot of money set aside for this purpose, but reliant on the revenue received by the Exchequer from current tax payers, both individual and corporate. The worry we face is that the money we pay in taxes is insufficient to meet the impending costs of the pension and health entitlements that we have come to expect.[10] These issues have become pressing, but governments of all shades find it difficult to address these runaway aspects of our taken-for-granted social provision. Governments duck and dive in relation to the challenge because the electoral implications would be immediate. Those who benefit from the status quo, i.e. older people, are therefore protected by their virtually unassailable electoral advantage.

The morality of democracy?

Peter G. Peterson, a US politician also highlights, like David Willetts in the UK, how democracy finds it difficult to take account of younger generations. Peterson reports on his conversations with George W. Bush while Bush was Governor of Texas. Peterson spoke of his concern about the viability of US entitlement (welfare) programs. He made the case that entitlement reform was both a philosophical and moral issue. It was a philosophical issue because modern, media-driven democracy focuses only on immediate crises, and though a free media was an essential aspect of democracy, it begged the question whether democracy could respond effectively to a very different kind of threat: a silent, slow motion, long-term crisis like entitlements.

George W. Bush, keen to put tax cuts at the heart of his forthcoming Presidential campaign, asked why social security and other entitlements could not be a lesser priority. Peterson provided the Governor with statistics relating to taxation and the huge debt the US would be passing on to future generations. He told Governor Bush that 'looking out for our children's future was a definitive test of the nation's morality,' and went on to suggest that this should take priority over tax cuts. Peterson describes how Governor Bush 'visibly stiffened as if he were hit in the gut, and responded, 'I don't think tax cuts are immoral'. Peterson replied: 'Governor, I didn't say long-term tax cuts were immoral. I said they were immoral until we have taken care of our long-term obligations to our children.'[11]

This question of how to honour the future is becoming ever more pressing, and it exposes a fault line in relation to free democratic decision-making which is considered to be the touchstone for a civilized society. The problem is how to balance political power in a society where demography has created a substantial group of people with the same interests. If democratic freedom is to be upheld, and the rights of future generations also upheld, then major moral readjustments will need to be made by a significant proportion of the electorate. In the face of this critical structural fault at the heart of democracy, and the apparent ignoring of its significance, the former US Treasury Secretary, Larry Summers, was heard to quip 'the only thing we have to fear is the lack of fear itself.'[12]

What has suddenly come on to the agenda of western nations is the possibility of not having enough money to meet future commitments. This anxiety has developed because of the money spent on bailing out the banks, which is said to be small compared to the fall in tax revenues associated with the ensuing economic recession. This has prompted major spending reviews to curb public expenditure. However, even without the financial crisis we have been living on borrowed time as well as borrowed resources. Anatole Kaletsky writes,

'Because of the promises on health and pensions made by successive governments all over the world to the ageing baby-boom generation, a fiscal crisis would have occurred sooner or later even in the absence of the 2008 meltdown. But the credit crunch brought forward this fiscal crisis by ten or 15 years.'[13]

It is important to note that what is being described is not just a problem for the United Kingdom. It is an issue for all the nations that are in or approaching the stage of 'advanced modernity'. In fact, in comparison with many nations, Britain is less severely affected by the imbalance between future obligations and anticipated tax revenues than most other nations. For example, the old-age dependency ratio[14] is anticipated to rise more in other countries such as the US, France, Germany, Italy and most notably in Japan and China. This is because the UK labour force is projected to grow by 16 per cent over the next 50 years compared with a 10% *contraction* across the European Union.[15] Although this gives the potential for more tax-payers in the UK, this will only bring a benefit if the amount of remunerated work expands to harness the capacity of upcoming workers.

ELDERLY PEOPLE IN CHINA[16]

Confucianism encourages respect for older people. Younger people are expected to defer to their elders by letting them speak first, sitting down after them and not contradicting them. People are often introduced from oldest to youngest. When offering a book or paper to someone older than you, you should use two hands to show respect.

The mandatory retirement age is 60 for men and 50 for women. Only 15 per cent of those that retire have pensions. Rural peasants generally don't receive any pensions. They are taken care of by their families. While there is plenty of scope to defer the retirement age, many companies want employees to retire early so they can employ younger people with IT skills.

The greying of the population

A consequence of the one-child policy is that the Chinese population is ageing rapidly, and this means that China is the first nation to have to cope with a population that is getting older before it becomes rich. In Shanghai people over 60 already make up 21.6 per cent of the population and are expected to make up 34 per cent in 2020. Similar trends are occurring across the country, especially in urban areas where the working-age population is expect to peak in about 2015.

Caring for elderly people is the law

A law was passed in 1996 stipulating that children are responsible for taking care of their parents in old age. Those who don't can face up to five years in jail. In Shanghai a neighbourhood committee decided to fine adult children who failed to invite their parents to celebrate Chinese New Year with them. Another committee posted the names and faces of those who did not visit their parent at least once every three months.

There are contests for those who are best at caring for their dependent relatives; state-run television runs drama series emphasizing the joy that comes from exercising one's filial responsibility.

We face a historically unique series of personal and family dilemmas about the way in which children in the future will express their filial responsibility – and how we 'here now' commit ourselves to unknown future generations. It is not just a question of scarcity of resources; it is also a question of how resources are distributed both between the generations and throughout the lifespan. It is also a challenge that exposes a fundamental weakness at the heart of the democratic process. The challenge confronts a particular generation of which I, and many others are members. Thurow puts the nature of the challenge this way,

'We have to generate values that allow us to go beyond the normal welfare calculus of capitalism to a mentality in which the satisfaction of building a better tomorrow outweighs the immediate appeal of greater and greater consumption.'[17]

The situation is stark: the longer we live the more likely we are to be the recipient of others' assets and this is a new moral problem that is now close at hand. We need all the imagination and generosity of spirit we can muster if we are to be able to respond adequately. This issue is of concern to all people of good will, but for people of faith, especially the Christian faith, we shall want to know what theology can offer to the struggle for future as well as present-day fairness.

Notes

1. The 'cougar' is slang for older women keen to date younger men. The term comes from a Canadian television series 'The Cougars' and the film 'The Cougar Club' (2007) and is now used widely on dating sites.
2. Rosamund Urwin 'The over–40s are stealing my golden years' in the *Evening Standard* 12 November 2009.
3. Vern L. Bengtson 'Is the 'Contract Across the Generations' Changing?' in *The Changing Contract Across the Generations,* eds V. L. Bengtson and W. A. Achenbaum (1993) New York: Aldine De Gruyter p. 4.
4. David Willets (2010) *The Pinch,* London: Atlantic Books p.23.
5. Based on Matthew 20 v.12.
6. Joseph Rowntree Foundation 'The Poverty Site' for UK statistics on poverty and social exclusion. http://www.poverty.org.uk/04/index.shtml
7. The 'welfare generation' could be said to involve those born in the early 1930s and up to and including the baby-boom generation. Although those born in the 1930s may have been born into great poverty, and had to endure the terrors and tragedies of a World War, they were also the generation that was well placed to take advantage of the opportunities associated with the period of demographic transition referred to in Chapter Two. They were youthful and in their prime during a period of full employment, low inflation and the unfurling of welfare provision.
8. P. Johnson, C. Conrad and D. Thomson (eds), (1989) *Workers versus Pensioners,* Manchester: Centre for Economic Policy Research (University of Manchester) p.7 (Introduction).
9. D. Thomson, 'The Welfare State and Generation Conflict: Winners and Losers' in *Workers versus Pensioners,* eds P. Johnson, C. Conrad and D. Thomson (1989) Manchester: Centre for Economic Policy Research (University of Manchester) p.45.
10. Some commentators, for example John Vincent, see a conspiracy in relation to pensions. He comments, 'The outcome of current debates and political conflicts over securing well-funded retirement turns out to be unexpectedly critical for the future of global capitalism.' He makes the case that the most cost-effective means of ensuring people have a pension in retirement is through government-run 'pay as you go' schemes, and that these would have remained affordable into the future. They also have the advantage of being relatively cheap to administer and provide governments with regular money. However, he argues that these clear advantages were sacrificed for the sake of the markets. By

discontinuing the government run universal earnings-related pension scheme, people were forced to invest in private pension schemes. These schemes run by large pension funds provide the major injection of new money into the markets. However, the risk associated with market investments is carried by individuals rather than the pension schemes or pension funds. See J. Vincent (2003) *Old Age*, London: Routledge pp 80–83 (quote p.80).

11. Peter G. Peterson (2004) *Running on Empty*, New York: Farrar, Straus and Giroux p. xxiv.
12. Ibid. p. xxvii.
13. Anatole Kaletsky 'Capitalism, but not as we know it' in *Prospect*, August 2010 p. 34.
14. The old-age dependency ratio is defined as the number of those of state pension age or above as a percentage of the working-age population.
15. European Commission (2009) *Ageing Report: Economic and budgetary projections for the EU–27 Member States*, Brussels: EU.
16. Based on Jeffrey Hays 'Elderly People in China' http://factsanddetails.com/china.php?itemid=106&catid=4&subcatid=21 and viewed on 28/7/2010.
17. L. C. Thurow 'The Birth of a Revolutionary Class', in *Generations Apart*, eds R. D. Thau and J. S. Heflin (1997) New York: Prometheus Books p. 35.

CHAPTER FOUR

Second chance theology

The gap between the rich and the poor is critical to the wellbeing of everyone, rich and poor alike. The research by Richard Wilkinson and Kate Pickett in their book 'The Spirit Level'[1] highlights the rather mysterious dynamics that suggest we are all inextricably linked together, regardless of our circumstances.[2] However, Wilkinson and Pickett in their research make an even more startling claim: We seem to have reached the end of the good things that economic growth can offer.

For thousands of years the best way of improving people's health and wellbeing has been through raising material living standards.[3] For ordinary people, throughout history, their lives have been plagued by hunger, thirst, disease and how to secure shelter from the elements. However, in sharp contrast, for the last two decades ordinary people have struggled to declutter all the stuff they have accumulated, or lose weight and get enough exercise. This is not a cheap dig at expanding waist lines. Just as there seems to be a collective dynamic that ties rich and poor together in the achievement of wellbeing and avoidance of misery, Wilkinson and Pickett's research also suggests the species Homo sapiens is at risk from having too many good things.

Wilkinson and Pickett's evidence suggests that at a certain point, as nations get richer and richer, increases in wellbeing and health begin to stall, and instead of happiness increasing, levels of anxiety and depression start to gain momentum. The discovery of this mysterious collective dynamic can in part be explained by what economists refer to as 'diminishing marginal utility', i.e. new products offer ever smaller benefits compared with the original item. For example, we are generally pleased to have fridges and washing machines, and better coffee, but while a fridge with a water chiller is an improvement, it is nowhere near as big an improvement as the shift from having a traditional larder to having a fridge. The ability to have a car with six rather than five gears may bring the boy racer some pleasure, but the thrill is unlikely to be as great as having a car for the first time; or moving from an Ipod Touch to an Ipod nano similarly brings diminishing benefits compared with the impact of the original.

In the far from trivial area of health care there are also discernible troubling dynamics. Despite vast energy and resources being ploughed into the health industry, the chances are that we have become the 'worried well' rather than brimming with health. Medical improvements may have increased to an unimagined degree, but this has served not to reassure, but to heighten anxiety, as we fret about whether we are getting the best treatment available or being fobbed off with what is to hand.

These examples are not, like Cassandra, offered to warn of impending and inevitable disaster. Rather, they are illustrations of Wilkinson and Pickett's thesis that, as nations get richer and richer, increases in wellbeing and health can stall, and anxiety and depression gain momentum. Even – or especially – in the face of ever improving technological conveniences and gadgets, and an ever widening range of choice, rather than being reassured and delighted we find ourselves under greater pressure and more careworn. The possibility really exists that too many good things can lead to misery rather than wellbeing.

When this thesis is applied to the generations the spectre of unfairness rises once again. The baby boomers appear to have had the best of times, benefiting from still high rather than diminishing levels of 'marginal utility'. Accordingly, wellbeing gained regular fillips in the context of confidence that, mostly, all was well with the world. In contrast, upcoming generations are exposed to the persuasions of the marketing industry that try to convince that the new model is substantially better that the old, only to find that the reality mostly disappoints. For younger and future generations technology has lost much of its capacity to thrill as the utility value falls and the triviality rises. In the face of this inevitable 'diminishing marginal utility', the ever adaptable market now fosters addiction, because addiction does not fall prey to diminishing marginal utility as each new fix is prized as much as the last. These addictions come in all shapes; most of them are unspeakable and shameful, and increasingly technology is used in their pursuit. Older generations, in comparison, have effortlessly enjoyed the 'cheap grace' of genuinely new things coming on the market, and have been spared the test of negotiating a path strewn with dastardly addictions.

An important piece of the jigsaw

Wilkinson and Pickett's thesis that nations that get richer and richer can find that gains in wellbeing and health stall, and that anxiety and depression gain momentum, provides an important jigsaw piece in the discernment of the sources of health and wellbeing. Demographers note that when the Industrial Revolution took hold, improvement in health and wellbeing was rooted in improvements in public health, in particular improvements in sanitation and the availability of clean water. In the 'modern' period in the second half of the twentieth century, gains in health and wellbeing have been due to improvements in medical skills and medication. The jigsaw piece from Wilkinson and Pickett suggests we have entered a third phase: a time when our health and wellbeing is linked with our *intentionality*, i.e. our intentional behaviour has an important bearing on whether we are healthy or unhealthy and whether our wellbeing is high or low. In other words, in a world of plenty, our health and wellbeing depend on our ability to avoid the hazards of addiction, to avoid eating the wrong food in the wrong amounts, and to have the willpower to embrace positive attitudes and actions.

The importance of intentionality or willpower comes as a shock to people of all ages; only the oldest of the generations have had practice in self-discipline that is at the heart of intentionality. In a world of too much and a culture of *selfish capitalism*, to use Oliver James' description, the ability to keep one's desires under control is critical. This is a very adult demand, because the essence of adulthood is being able to control one's impulsiveness and resist acting on the basis of unruly emotions and passions.

Affluenza?

Oliver James, the author of 'Affluenza – How to Be Successful and Stay Sane'[4], writes:

'I have discovered that citizens of English-speaking nations are twice as likely to suffer mental illness as ones from mainland Western Europe. Specifically, my analysis reveals that over a 12-month period nearly one-quarter (23 per cent) of English speakers suffered, compared with 11.5 per cent of mainland western Europeans... Selfish capitalism causes mental illness by spawning materialism, or, as I put it, the affluenza virus – by placing a high value on money, possessions, appearances (social and physical) and fame. English-speaking nations are more infected with the virus than mainland western European ones. Studies in many nations prove that people who strongly subscribe to virus values are at significantly greater risk of depression, anxiety, substance abuse and personality disorder.'[5]

Traditionally, religions have provided people with the motivation to control desire and unruly emotions and passions. But this has often been achieved by coercing those who stepped out of line and forcing people to behave themselves in a prescribed manner. The emotional bullying perfected by religious institutions to constrain both the thinking and the behaviour of individuals, and indeed of societies, brought a plague of guilt upon earlier generations. This combination of domineering religion, and the implausibility of some of the beliefs associated with religion, prompts many to despise religion and all things religious.

The expression of religion and the practice of religious institutions can change. Although religions often claim and are perceived to be dealing in absolutes, the manifestation or articulation of a religion is inevitably shaped by the wider culture in which it exists. In other words, the particular emphasis that religion takes is melded by the culture of the era. So the emphasis and practice that characterized the

Christian religion in Victorian and Edwardian times, and earlier 'Christendom',[6] is not the manner of the Christian faith today. Even so, given previous nasty performances of religion, it is asking a lot for people to give religion a second chance. However, just as there is second chance education for those who were let down by schooling and their education first time round, so too the plea is that religion, and in particular the Christian religion, is given a second hearing or second chance.

The desires at the heart of churches and their teaching have been transformed. No longer is the desire to sup with the powerful and see the world through the eyes of the powerful. Christians have come to lament this longstanding and profound misrepresentation of Jesus' life and teaching. This transformation means that Church is a different place, and Christian teaching different in emphasis from that which those outside the Church imagine. Churches and Christian theology have changed for the better and are worthy of a second hearing. This appeal for a second chance is not made for the sake of the churches. It is made for the sake of the future. The resources and clues that derive from Jesus' life and teaching are critically important if we are to act upon our concern for the future, and in the past these resources have been masked by the pre-occupation of the Church with the accumulation of power, and for this the established churches must ask forgiveness.

So what is new?

The contemporary gist of Christian teaching, engendered in part no doubt by a highly individualized society, encourages personal integrity as well as a strong sense of ego and the legitimacy of investing in our uniqueness. For example, Alison Webster writes:

'It is my conviction that our uniqueness is intended. It is a divine gift. We are meant to revel in it, to love ourselves and appreciate our glorious one-offness. To the extent that we embrace our uniqueness, God is delighted, and as we stretch out towards intimacy with others, God's passion is alight.'[7]

This idea that delight, intimacy and relishing our individuality are not just acceptable to God, but that God is desirous of us achieving this state, can be found frequently in contemporary theology. Contemporary Christianity, aided by the prevailing culture, has been set free from a series of 'oughts' and now encourages thoughtful choice in the pursuit of personal integrity. There should be neither shame nor surprise at this; there is no disgrace in theological thinking being informed by ideas from wider society. What would become disgraceful would be to deny or resist new ways of seeing and understanding that come our way, whether from our religious tradition, or secular insight, or from the Holy Spirit. However, there is a corollary to this. Contemporary theology, under the influence of the wider culture can drift beyond the endorsement of individualism, and expectation of 'life in all its fullness', and fail to recognize that its teaching and practice have given way to self-indulgence. With this caution, the contemporary shape of Christian theology provides valuable, even essential resources for navigating the tricky terrain of intergenerational fairness and attending to the rights of future generations.

Theology is mostly talk about God, but it is not just this. Theology also takes the human condition very seriously and honestly. Even for those who struggle to comprehend the idea of God there is affirmation from contemporary theology. The advice is to relax, to hold off efforts to figure out the possibility of God, because God is not to be comprehended; rather, we apprehend or stumble upon God, often in the most unexpected of ways. Contemporary Christian theology lauds faith rather than belief, and this means it gives value to the most hesitant sense that there is more to life that we can understand. In welcoming the most fragile intimation of the possibility of God, the door is opened to the most beautiful expression of longing and engaged hope that could be imagined. The efforts and inspiration of honest thinkers and humble souls through the generations combine to provide a fund of Gospel insights that help to make this earth a better place. I offer five elements from this precious fund:

- The legitimacy of achieving an appropriate sense of self and our place in the world, a sense of self that speaks of uniqueness and preciousness in the sight of God, and a place in the world that calls us to commit ourselves to the struggle for the earth's future flourishing, and the flourishing of all that today dwells therein.
- An imperative towards compassion, which means a willingness to put others' interests ahead of our own.
- Recognition of the conscious and unconscious dastardliness that permeates all we do, and the importance of traditional spiritual practices in lessening the impact of our dastardliness, including shedding the ingrained habit of blaming and scapegoating others.
- Recognition of the importance and availability of forgiveness, spoken of and enacted by Jesus, both as an aspect of good mental health and as a contributor to personal and communal resilience.
- Confidence 'That all shall be well and all manner of things shall be well' because of the love of God enfolding the Creation.

Sin

Systems view

60

These five themes are commended as practical theology i.e. a theology that can be performed and practised and which we can aspire to achieve. These themes form much of what it means to follow Jesus. In making every effort to *perform* (behave) in ways that are shaped by these considerations, the emphasis on belief as the key dimension of the Christian faith is lessened. Instead, the emphasis shifts to the flow between understanding and action, with each informing the other. These five themes are drawn from the array of teachings and doctrines from the Christian tradition and the Biblical canon. They are offered as a constellation[8] that can enable us to negotiate the mounting complexities and pressures we face. These five themes are also commended because of their resonance with the zeitgeist of our time. They are not too distant from the best of humanistic values and nor are they bound by the hard to believe formularies of a tightly systematic faith that is beyond the ken of those who, at best, can only half believe. Nevertheless, I suggest that despite this very gentle gradient in the direction of orthodox Christian teaching, these themes do justice to the essence of the faith that has Jesus at its heart.

Compassionate intentionality

This constellation is offered as a foundation for intentionality; it is meant to inform and shape our *performance*. Intentionality is that stage before action or behaviour; it is that stage where we pre-figure our actions and it is critical to our eventual performance. We will all be accustomed to the possibility, even the likelihood, of our actions or behaviour falling short of our intentions. This may be put down to a lack of skill or motivation, or a lack of self-discipline, or a combination of all these things.

However, if justice is to be rolled out into the future, then our intentionality and our eventual performance need to be in sync – at least for much of the time. To achieve this we need to be resilient, meaning that we can recover from setbacks. It is in relation to this that second chance theology, or the five-point constellation spelt out above, is to be prized. The assurance of forgiveness, an imagination informed by far-ranging compassion, commitment to resist blaming others and a deep confidence that the struggle is not in vain: all these need to become the *habits of the heart* if we are to be fit for the struggle.

This poetic expression 'habits of the heart' was used by Tocqueville, the French social philosopher, in his pioneering analysis of the powerful interplay between character and society in 1830s America. In 1985, 150 years later, Robert Bellah and his colleagues re-visited Tocqueville's perceptions and investigated how the 'habits of the heart' of ordinary Americans had changed. Their findings led them to conclude that individualism may have grown so extensive and deep that it was like a cancer, eating up the bonds that held American society together.[9] Tocqueville himself had previously noted the threat carried by excessive individualism. He wrote:

'Individualism is a calm and considered feeling which disposes each citizen to isolate himself from the mass of his fellows and withdraw into the circle of family and friends. Within this little society, formed to his taste, he gladly leaves the greater society to look after itself.'[10]

Tocqueville goes on:

'Such folk owe no man anything and hardly expect anything from anybody. They form the habit of thinking of themselves in isolation, and imagine that their whole destiny is in their hands.'[11]

Finally, Tocqueville comments directly on the issue at hand. Those caught up in the momentum towards individualism:

'Forget their ancestors and descendants …each man is forever thrown back on himself alone, and there is a danger that he may be shut up in the solitude of his own heart'.[12]

Bellah and his team, and Tocqueville before them, documented how deep and extensive individualism corrodes both wellbeing and civil society, and weakens our capacity for wider commitment because of being *shut up in our own heart*. This 'aloneness' of individualism has two major consequences:

- The basis for the values and priorities that we construct for ourselves is likely to be what we ourselves happen to find rewarding. When we construct our values and priorities without reference to others, we are unlikely to be able to justify or give an account of them in relation to any wider purpose or belief framework.
- There is a disincentive towards compassionate behaviour, because only a fool would risk being committed to the wellbeing of others in a context where everyone else is pursuing his or her own interests.

This description by Tocqueville of being 'shut up in the solitude of our own heart' frames the choices that all of us face, and I would say especially those approaching their third age. We meet a crossroad: the option is to continue with withdrawal into one's narrow circle of family and friends as

Tocqueville described; or the option of exploring the imperative towards compassion, and risk putting others' interests ahead of one's own.

Living life for one's self, and with no higher vision of human flourishing than that of self-interest, is the subject of one of Jesus' best known sayings: 'The man who would save his life will lose it, and the person who gives up his life for the sake of others will find his life.' Today researchers in the field of positive psychology[13] would reach the same conclusion. Their research repeatedly demonstrates that having a sense of purpose that is pitched wider than self-interest is the route to wellbeing. Shorn of such a commitment to a wider and greater purpose, the capacity for self-forgetfulness is lost, and those who can think of nothing other than their personal self-interest are likely to be sad and frustrated as well as unfulfilled.

In a culture that encourages a high degree of individualism, experimenting with compassionate intentionality requires both significant moral stretch as well as personal agency. The capacity to put aside self-preoccupation and self-interest is a vocation particularly for older people, because having forged one's identity and status there is room for a more gracious performance. Such an enterprise, especially in relation to the challenge of extending justice into the future, and its consequence, minimizing the degree to which we borrow from the future, has sharp edges because it is deeply personal, and it makes particular demands on the imagination and compassion of the baby boom generation.

Church matters

Having risked alienating those readers with little or no faith by commending a constellation of theological thoughts, I go a step further and risk commending the church as a resource for helping us to make sense of our lives and to find fellow travellers trying to live lives of compassionate intentionality.

The progress from intention to actual performance is fraught with slip-ups – ask anyone who tries to diet. However, ask a member of an AA or Gamblers' Anonymous Group, or a member of Weight Watchers, what the secret is of ensuring continuity between intentionality and the desired behaviour, and they will reply that the support of others is essential. Solidarity in the struggle is not just a political strapline. A church is a place where intentionality is discerned and refreshed, and supported and renewed. But even more than this, the church at local, national and international level is a resource which enables campaigns to be launched and sustained. If fairness and justice are to be secured for the future, then more than individual acts of generosity and compassion are needed. Despite the fact that being a churchgoer in Britain is to be part of a hard-pressed and sometimes fragile collective, churches, more than any other network in Britain, have the proven capacity to become a movement for change.

Susan George's Observations on Jubilee 2000

Susan George is a long term analyst of globalization and its impact on the poor. Based in France she speaks from a secular perspective. Writing in her book *Another world is possible if...*, she notes the significance of Jubilee 2000:

'From the late 1990s on, a powerful international campaign against Third World debt called Jubilee 2000 collected millions of signatures and held successful mass actions involving tens of thousands of people. In 1998, 70,000 of them congregated to form a human chain ('Make a chain to break the chains of debt') to tell Tony Blair's G7 summit in Birmingham that it must act on the issue.

Jubilee 2000 went far beyond the traditional Left and brought in people who had never marched on a demo in their entire lives. I know, because I was in Birmingham and asked many of them. The campaign took its name from the biblical notion of Jubilee, or periodic forgiveness of debts, and was particularly well positioned in the Church. The millennium year 2000 was to be the year the chains were broken and the debt captives set free. And this campaign did force politicians of the G7, the world's richest countries, to act'. [14]

In relation to justice and fairness between the generations, the need for collective thinking and action is pressing. Even a shared language to describe the concepts at the heart of the issue remains to be created, and until this is done the task of consciousness raising is impossible. Without this, concern about how to take care of the future gets limited to the realm of private anxiety. The formation of a *collective* to begin this early work is essential. However, political parties are unlikely to invest in this long-term goal – for the reasons identified in chapter three – and trades unions likewise have a vested interest in relation to particular generations. What remains are the churches and other faith-related organizations. Reliance on the churches is not as hopeless as the secular world would like to think. The churches in particular, despite discouragement, know how to position themselves in the public arena.

Community or Citizens' Organizing is an example of the adeptness of churches and faith-related organizations to engage with and unlock the power of civil society for the common good, and potentially for the good of the future.

Community or Citizens' Organizing is a movement that has been around for over forty years, beginning with Saul Alinsky in Chicago. The first to give financial backing to Alinsky's organization was the Catholic Diocese of Chicago, and ever since churches and faith-related organizations have been in the vanguard. This is not just the case in the US; it is likewise the case in relation to Citizens' UK.

The aim of Citizens' Organizing is to mobilize people to act on their passion for justice. Sometimes these are local issues and sometimes they are issues of national concern. For example, in the UK people have been mobilized in relation to the Living Wage Campaign, the creation of land trusts, and 'Strangers into Citizens', a campaign to provide a route to citizenship for irregular migrants. So far 'Organizing' has focused on spreading justice 'here now' but it has the potential to embrace 'justice into the future', and mobilize and give voice to the compassionate intentionality that is coming to birth in relation to concern for younger and future generations.

Alasdair MacIntyre is one of the world's most influential living moral philosophers. His most famous book *After Virtue*[15] has a stark and unexpected ending. In the book he warns about our preoccupation with the accumulation of money, power and status, which he fears will lead us into a new age of 'darkness and barbarism'. He concludes his forceful analysis by offering just the single suggestion about the recovery of virtue: the need for another St Benedict. St Benedict provided a rule and structures to help translate compassionate intentionality into dependable and sustainable action. He did this through the development of monasteries as far back as the sixth century (although there are records of monasteries as far back as the fourth century), and his rules of life both for individuals and in relation to the running of a monastery are still used today.

MacIntyre is not suggesting the return to monastic life, but he is commending a concerted and corporate effort to discipline our desires in the direction of virtue, or what second chance theology might call *compassionate intentionality*. Churches may be as good as it gets in relation to persistent communities willing to struggle with such an alternative intentionality and alternative performance – for the sake of the future.

Notes

1. R. Wilkinson and K. Pickett (2010) *The Spirit Level*, London: Penguin Books.
2. There are challenges to the Wilkinson and Pickett research, sometimes on the grounds of cherry-picking from the vast array of statistics in order to support their theory, or underestimating the impact of national cultures, especially between Anglo-Saxon and Scandinavian nations. The challenges come from the work of N. Sanandaji, A. Malm and T. Sanandaji (2010) *The Spirit Illusion*, web publication by the Taxpayers' Alliance *http://www.taxpayersalliance. com/spiritillusion.pdf*; and P. Saunders (2010) *Beware False Prophets: Equality, the Good Society and The Spirit Level*, London: The Policy Exchange.
3. This long period (across two centuries) is to be distinguished from the 'demographic window' linked with the fourth stage of the theory of demographic transition in which there is the possibility of a 'demographic dividend' in relation to economic growth. This occurs when the proportion of dependent youngsters is low compared to the number of working people in the population.
4. Oliver James (2007) *Affluenza*, London: Vermilion.
5. Oliver James 'Infected by Affluenza', the *Guardian* 24 January 2007.
6. The term 'Christendom' is used to describe that long period of European history (although not limited to Europe) when religious thinking and religious institutions were the power in the land. Christians today increasingly lament this inheritance because of how it has added to people's resentment of religion, and how it profoundly misrepresents what is at the heart of the Gospel.
7. Alison Webster (2009) *You Are Mine*, London: SPCK p.6.

8. The essence of a constellation is that it is a pattern which is identified within a vast array of stars. Applying the idea of 'constellation' to theology is to define a pattern of interrelated ideas that can be lifted from the vast array of theological ideas that are available to us. It does not mean that other ideas are dismissed or invalidated. John Drane uses the idea of 'jazz' in relation to the vast wealth of theological ideas as a way of emphasizing a particular riff that grabs the attention and becomes a theme that gets taken up with variations.

9. R. N. Bellah, R. Madsen, W. M. Sullivan, A. Swidler and S. M. Tipton (1985) *Habits of the Heart*, Berkeley; University of California Press p.vii.

10. A. de Tocqueville (1969) *Democracy in America*, trans. G. Lawrence, ed. J. P. Mayer, New York: Doubleday, p.506.

11. Ibid. p.508.

12. Ibid p.510.

13. Positive Psychology is a recent branch of psychology that focuses on the things that contribute to human flourishing and wellbeing. In other words, the focus of study is what is going right rather than wrong in individuals and societies, thus shifting away from the focus of some psychologists, for example, on mental illness. Martin Seligman is credited with being the founder of this approach.

14. S. George (2004) *Another world is possible if...*, London: Verso p. 193.

15. A. MacIntrye, (1984) *After Virtue*, Notre Dame: University of Notre Dame Press.

CHAPTER FIVE

Age has its purpose?

This chapter has two purposes:

- To highlight the positives that come with age in order to give value to age, not just for individuals but for society itself.
- To emphasize how those who are old now are pioneers, having to explore new terrain with an out-of-date map.

In relation to the issue of intergenerational fairness, the point of the chapter is to cry aloud 'Don't shoot your granny', not just for her sake but for your own. The relationships between the generations, especially those between older and younger generations, have been hard won by Homo sapiens, and the possibility of resentment unravelling this crucial inter-relationship has to be resisted.

Those whom we think of as old are almost always someone else rather than us. Talking about age is a tricky business, not just because we often avoid owning up to our age, but because we often have only a tentative sense of having become old. Without a mirror, and spared too many aches and pains, we can easily fancy ourselves as little more than thirty-five ... or forty. Some part of us naturally resists the ageing process and remains untouched; deep inside us there is a 'self' that remains young. This experience of the distance between one's interior age and the age we see when we look in the mirror, and to which others respond, is described as the 'mask of ageing'[1], and perhaps this mask is as old as humankind itself.

From an old photograph album

'Dad. A dark haired man in baggy pants and a wide-brimmed hat. And mother. A sad-eyed woman in a print dress. I look back at them, dressed in their Depression and Wartime clothes, and I realize that those images are burned deeply into my consciousness. They are more than memories. They are images of what Adults – real Grown-Ups – are like. As I look at them, it occurs to me with a shock that somewhere in the back of my mind I was still waiting for adulthood to arrive... When I came to be my father's age, I dressed and cut my hair differently. I never grew up into that smiling man in the rimless glasses and with white pants, the one leaning carelessly back against the '36 Plymouth Coupé. He is the real adult. I'm an impostor.'[2]

Today the 'way markers' in relation to old age have become more and more vague. Those who are in their sixties are usually pretty clear that they are not old, despite the fact that throughout the *whole* of human history to have reached the age of sixty was to have reached decrepitude. But that's not how it is today. As longevity increases we can light-heartedly announce that sixty is the new forty and any idea of being old can be put off for another decade. The fact that it is normal to live to our eighties, and that we can do so without being waylaid by too many of the diminishments and hazards associated with ageing, gives even more encouragement to distance ourselves from old age. Even if we do get waylaid by physical hazards, the chances are there is a medical fix that sorts things out for us. So at sixty-eight… this can't be old age yet? Can it? This query is not just about denial, it is a genuine puzzle, because the experience we have today of ageing is profoundly different from what it has been for the full stretch of human history.

Even though the *bodily reminders* of our age may be increasingly fallacious in cueing us to act our chronological age, Karp[3] lists other cues that prompt us to act our age. There are *generational reminders*, for example being at the wedding of one's granddaughter, or the funeral of one's last remaining brother or sister: these things conspire to give a sense of getting older and becoming old. There are *contextual reminders*. For example, I have mixed emotions when someone offers me their seat on the bus as I get cued by others into age-appropriate behaviour. Ultimately, Karp recognizes that we may also get the powerful cue from 'our own *sense of mortality*'; this might be a sudden heart attack or stroke, or a diagnosis of dementia or cancer. As we move from early to late (or deep) old age, we are likely to trigger all these four cues, and ultimately ageing has to be acknowledged as the process by which we daily come closer to death.

Although there are these cues that prompt us to act our age, more than ever before we are likely to be disorientated. Having gleaned our view of ageing from the experience of our parents and grandparents, the likelihood is that our judgement about ageing will be a decade off target. The speed with which the lifespan has extended over a single generation is unknown in human history, so it is understandable that we are disorientated and prone to get ahead of ourselves. Until the last sixty years it was a fair assumption that our lives, if we were lucky, would have three stages: childhood into adolescence, building our own family, followed by the relinquishing of prowess associated with old age. This perception of the life course has been around since time immemorial (Figure 1), but suddenly it has become wide of the mark because our lives do not take this shape any more.

This three-stage model of life, that has persisted for aeons, has become redundant within a single generation. There are deeply ingrained assumptions associated with this three-stage

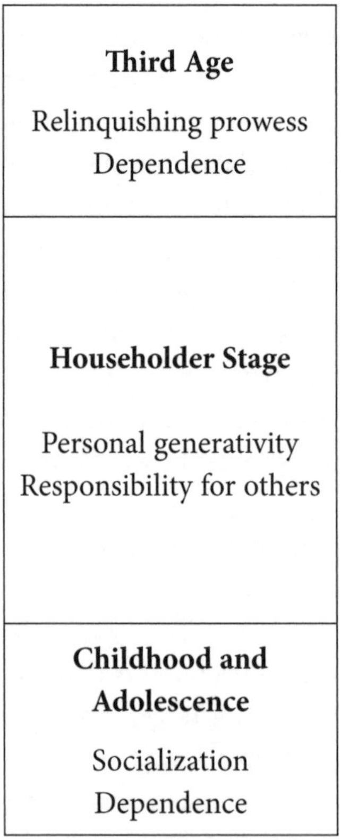

Third Age

Relinquishing prowess
Dependence

Householder Stage

Personal generativity
Responsibility for others

**Childhood and
Adolescence**

Socialization
Dependence

Figure 1

view of the lifespan. We habitually assume that the three stages in the life span are not just different, but that the second stage is better than the other two. The second or middle stage is the *pinnacle* of life – when we are assumed to be in our prime or at the peak of our potential. This second stage is followed by 'falling off the pace' and inevitable *decline* into the third and final stage of life – this is old age.

Throughout the whole of human history we have accepted this pattern of the lifespan, but now we have to shake off this traditional view, because if we don't we risk squandering the extraordinary gift of years that has befallen those born in the 1930s, 40s and 50s. This age cohort, as Peter Laslett emphasizes, is the generation of pathfinders exploring a *fresh map of life,*[4] because for the first time in human history our map of life consists not of three stages, but four. (Figure 2)

In this new map of life, the second stage of life, the stage that is usually associated with creating our own household,[5] which technically is referred to as *generativity*, is followed by a new third age. It is new because no longer is this third age about letting go of prowess. Loss of prowess and capacity in this new four-stage map of life, belongs to the fourth age. This fourth age, is most likely to be the shortest stage in the lifespan, lasting on average only four years – the final years of our life. If we can expect to live well into our eighties, this leaves the *third* age stretching for twenty or more years.

Peter Laslett, who was one of the first to acknowledge this new shape to our lives, writes:

'All our ageing expressions have become inaccurate, and many of them obsolete. They provide us with misleading images of children, adults, those in the prime of life, a

75

Fourth Age Relinquishing prowess Dependence
Third Age ?
Householder Stage Personal generativity Responsibility for others
Childhood and **Adolescence** Socialization Dependence

Figure 2

phrase to be noted because we are going to shift the prime of life a long way towards the later years. For the age constitution of our society has been transformed, quite suddenly and without our realizing what has happened… We need a new outlook, a new language, and we need above all, a new institution or set of institutions.'[6]

The suddenness with which this new shape to our lives has come about makes it unsurprising that we fumble for ways of making sense of this apparent gift of extra years. Even the usually acute alertness and sure-footedness of the media seem clumsy and unsure how to portray this new third age: Grumpy 'One Foot in the Grave' or the devil may care 'Golden Girls'? But the media have a great incentive to get up to speed, because older people form almost a third of the population and form almost half of those who have money to spare; therefore they are of interest to advertisers with products to sell. The need to take the ageing of our population seriously is not an option, it is essential, because advanced modern societies will never be young again.

Evolutionary advantage

Homo sapiens has always been a species that potentially lives for a long time. For example, zoologists estimate that human beings live twice as long as our nearest relative in the animal kingdom. Biologists confirm that the processes of evolution are ultra-efficient. Developments occur and spread within a species because they have survival value for members of the species, unless the species becomes addicted to some destructive patterns of behaviour. This exacting dynamic is the essence of evolution, and from it we can deduce that Homo sapiens would not live as long as it does if this longevity had no purpose. This purpose provides a compass point to help negotiate the fresh map of life.

William Thomas describes the advantages that accrue to Homo sapiens as a result of the availability of the unencumbered older female. He describes the likely plight of a hominid child, born a million years ago on the plains of Africa:

'Her mother has recently given birth and is distracted by the needs of her helpless infant... the mother barely has the strength to nurse the infant. She can neither feed nor care for her older child. The mother of the new mother, the grandmother of the crying child, is the first to act. Thus the first tentative step taken down the long road that led to the development of the modern human being. The deliberate enlistment of grandparents into the work of rearing the young stands out as a defining characteristic of Homo sapiens.'[7]

Although the longevity of Homo sapiens is greater than that of our nearest relative, the chimpanzee, the decades of fertility for females of both species remain similar; both human females and chimpanzee females remain fertile for around four decades. However, for the aged chimp, soon after the loss of fertility her metabolism closes down quite rapidly and death follows. In contrast, the human female can expect forty to fifty years longevity after she has lost fertility. Robert D. Martin, a zoologist, suggests that this extraordinary longevity of the female of the species beyond her fertility must be linked with the contribution that older females make to the rearing of the next but one generation. He suggests that the social environment the young offspring has to negotiate is too complex to be mediated by the parenting generation alone,[8] and needs to be nuanced by the older generation.

There are other benefits that have accrued to the species Homo sapiens from the availability of unencumbered elders.

For example, in the time of hunter gatherers, some fifty thousand years ago, there was a very basic equation: youngsters ate more than they could hunt or gather, adults probably ate as much as they hunted and gathered, older women ate less than they could gather, and so the enduring capacity of older women compensated for what would otherwise be a recurring shortfall.[9]

Why do women live longer than men?

Even today, when longevity of both men and women has increased substantially, women continue to live on average five years longer than men. The Oxford based gerontologist Sir John Grimley-Evans suggests two things have brought this about. The first is that men, especially young men, are greater risk takers than women and are less likely to settle into a regular and healthy pattern of life, and this eats into men's longevity.

The second factor is more intriguing and goes back to the days of hunter gatherers. Women were the gatherers and men were the hunters. While the berries and leaves gathered by women might sustain the group through hard times, it was the meat, the protein, which would provide the real boost to the group. It would be the women who would cook and distribute the food, always ensuring that the men had enough before taking their own share.

There were two reasons for this: first, it was imperative that the men remained strong because, if their capacity failed, the group would be starved of protein and all would weaken. The second reason was because one of the earliest forms of birth control was to lower one's intake of food, even at the risk of malnourishment. What might not have been anticipated by those women of fifty thousand years ago was that their repeated experience of hunger would trigger their immune system. As a result of relying on the food that was left, regardless of how meagre, women's immune system has been forced into overdrive more frequently than men's. This has brought an extraordinary benefit to women: women's immune system is more robust than men's, and this is reflected not just in the greater longevity of women compared to men, but also in the different perinatal[10] mortality rate of the sexes: significantly more boys die in the first year of life compared with girls.

Elderhood

William Thomas, in promoting the idea that older people make a distinctive contribution to the flourishing of the species, suggests that even the physiological changes associated with old age have a special purpose. The aching joints, fading eyesight and all the other debilities associated with later life provide an incentive to older people to forego the active life and embrace the home-based tasks of caring for children and the formation of the young adult. And more even than this, he suggests that the physical limitations that encroach with the decades bring with them an inclination towards peace-making, including gains such as moral courage, forgiveness and empathy, attributes that make peace a possibility. Such aptitudes and inclinations become a priceless contribution in the context of tribal feuds and family disputes.

The oldest are the first to leave

Jesus was suddenly confronted by the Pharisees and teachers of the Law. They had dragged before him a woman who had been caught in the act of adultery. They tell Jesus what he already knows: that the Jewish Law requires her to be stoned, and they ask him what he says to this. It is a trap; he either damns the woman or damns himself. We read that he takes his time, thinks for a while and replies that it should be the person without sin who casts the first stone.[11] We read that gradually the woman's accusers slink off – starting with the oldest.

This Gospel story highlights two things: the dastardliness of the species Homo sapiens and the important role of old people. Stoning was the equivalent of a lynching in the Wild West. However, there was a potential strand of dignity and decency that pervaded this unholy and self-righteous mob-handedness. It would be the oldest of those gathered who had the power to direct the action. The convention was that it was the oldest who had the greatest capacity to exercise judgement. In relation to this story from John ch. 8, it was the oldest who was first to get the point Jesus was making. It was the oldest of the Pharisees and Teachers of the Law who were the first to discern and convey the message to others that judgement was not theirs to carry out.

If you have trained as a teacher you will be familiar with the work of Piaget. Piaget died in 1980 having set up a centre in Geneva to study developmental psychology. As a young man he had spent time marking intelligence tests for the famous Alfred Binet. Piaget noticed that there was a pattern to the questions that young children got wrong. This led him to his theory that young people's cognitive[12] processing was different from that of adults. From this insight he went on to propose (and test) his theory that as we move from birth into childhood and then into adulthood, we all go through distinctive stages of cognition, the final stage of which Piaget called 'formal operations'.

Formal operations require the ability to handle abstract ideas, harnessing a capacity for logical reasoning and systematic planning. In more down-to-earth terms, formal operations means that a person can think about a problem or option, analyse it, form hypotheses, then reason whether or not a particular response is a good idea. Piaget thought that most adolescents achieved the capacity for formal operations by their late teens, and he considered the achievement of formal operations as the final stage of the cognitive development of Homo sapiens. Piaget writes:

'(Formal operations) constitute a complex but coherent system, relatively different from the logic of the child: it constitutes the essence of the logic of educated adults, as well as the basis of the elementary forms of scientific thought.'[13]

Following the lead given by Piaget, developmental psychology focused on childhood and adolescence because of this assumption that all cognitive development is achieved in the first twenty years of life. Klaus Riegal was one of the first developmental psychologists who explored the possibility of a stage beyond Piaget's formal operations that represented adult thinking more accurately. He termed this the stage of dialectical operations. For Riegel, rather than focusing on right answers and formal reasoning, the dialectical thought which he considered to characterize maturity involves the capacity to hold together or integrate apparent contradictions, and rather than be troubled by these contradictions, to be energized by them and allow them to provide a foundation for creativity and compassion.[14]

For Riegal, and other developmental psychologists interested in post-formal thinking, the most distinctive and salient features of mature adult thinking are:

- Appreciation of the relativistic nature of knowledge i.e. context has to be taken into account.
- Acceptance of contradiction as a non-reducible component of life, i.e. a permanent feature of life.
- Integration of contradiction by embracing a larger and more inclusive frame of reference.

The poet John Keats arrives at a more elegant description of the dialectical operations identified by developmental psychologists. He writes of our capacity for 'negative capabilities' and he describes this capability as 'when a man is capable of being in uncertainties, mysteries, doubts, without any irritable reaching after fact and reason.'[15]

Wisdom = Dialectical operations?

'Unschooled people can acquire wisdom, and it is no more common to find wise people among professors than it is among carpenters, fishermen or housewives. Wherever it exists, wisdom shows itself as a perception of the relativity and relationship among things. It is an awareness of wholeness which does not lose sight of particularity or concreteness, or the intricacies of interrelationships. It is where the left- and right-hand brains come together in a union of the logic and poetry and sensation, and where self-awareness is no longer at odds with awareness of the otherness of the world.'[16]

If, as the developmental psychologists suggest, the way in which we think and understand the world continues to develop throughout life, then this has two implications:

- Rather than assume that the challenge as we grow older is to maintain a mid-life pattern of activity for as long as we can, the achievement of 'dialectical operations' in later life makes possible a redefinition of self and our relationship with others, as well as a greater capacity for engaging with existential questions to do with the purpose and meaning of life.

• Drawing on the insights from biologists and zoologists described earlier, if a species has developed a distinctive thinking or cognitive style associated with elderhood, then this must be of some positive benefit to the species.

Here the seminal work of Erik Erikson comes into its own. In his analysis of the lifespan, Erikson, like Riegel, identified specific developmental stages and associated tasks that run throughout our lives, including later life. Erikson suggests that in mature or late adulthood, the principal task is to guide the next generation, and failure to act on this brings stagnation. In one leap Erikson answers the question about the purpose of the extensive 'third age', which is the distinctive element in the fresh map of life referred to earlier (Figure 2). Erikson writes,

'If there is any responsibility in the cycle of life, it must be that one generation owes to the next that strength by which it can come to face ultimate concerns in its own way – unmarred by debilitating poverty or by neurotic concerns caused by emotional exploitation.'[17]

Elsewhere Erikson, unafraid to use the term wisdom, comments,

'The virtue we can develop in old age is wisdom, that detached concern with life itself in the face of death itself. It (wisdom) maintains and conveys the integrity of experience, in spite of the decline in bodily and mental functions. It responds to the need of the oncoming generation for an integrated heritage and yet remains aware of the relativity of all knowledge.'[18]

If more confirmation is needed that the special 'gifting' of elderhood is for some purpose, there are other potential, distinctive attributes associated with later life, in addition to the capacity for dialectical operations, and these also point to the exceptional contribution that older people can make to the flourishing of future generations. For example:

- Greater ability to *be in the present.* This may seem counter-intuitive as older people are characterized by the inclination to focus on the past. To an extent this may be so, but this urge for a backward look is nothing compared with the extent to which youth and the middle aged focus on the future. The urge to prefigure the future, trying on for size possible future selves and planning for the future, is a rarely acknowledged preoccupation of those in the early and mid stages of the lifespan. The capacity to be 'here now', to use counselling jargon, is hugely important in providing steady and patient attentiveness. In relation to spirituality it is also a boon, because the ability to 'be attentive to the present moment' is the foundation for contemplating the 'ground of all being', to use Paul Tillich's phrase.
- The slur of eccentricity falls away. This is what is at the heart of the most popular poem about the third age: 'Warning – When I am an old woman I shall wear purple' by Jenny Joseph. The comic attributes listed in the poem, such as running one's stick along the railings, and eating three pounds of sausages at a go, cloak a profound series of benefits. When

we are unafraid of people's opinion of us then the likelihood is that we relax our defences. This has the effect of releasing the emotional energy that would otherwise be devoted to managing the way in which we present ourselves to others. When free of the need to create the right impression, one can be less defended, and this release of energy gets transformed into an increase in one's resilience and stamina.

- A related gain is that as we age we are likely to reduce the number of different roles we have. This helps ego integration as we face up to the challenge of *who and how we are to be*. Basically, there are no longer as many hiding or pretending places! This contributes to authenticity and in a postmodern world, where judgements are no longer based on explicit values, authenticity is the criterion for judging someone as sound.

- Ego integration frees us from the persistent, demanding ego needs that in earlier stages of life might lead to jealousy, unhealthy competitiveness and the danger of undermining those who get in our way. In part this attribute develops because of retirement from employment, and the urge to be a success subsides, and it becomes more fulfilling to *make a contribution*. This reduction in one's ego needs means that it becomes more likely that one relates to others in an open, consistent and humane way.

- The movement away from employment does not mean that competence is lost, although the context in which one can deliver one's competence may well have gone. Competence remains and to it can be added *availability*. This is an extraordinary resource that cries out for more opportunities for older people to contribute to society.

- In the later stage of life there is the scope to discover some good, wholesome dependencies. When we recognize the many ways in which we are dependent on each other, and the systems that sustain our lifestyle, we become more alert to the tiny capillaries that carry the obligations between millions of strangers. Never before in human history have we been so dependent on myriad, interconnected systems working smoothly for our benefit. This glimpse of how everything is connected to everything else provides a foundation for generosity, humility and gratitude: the triune pillars of strong relationships and civic responsiveness.

The availability of time is what is usually associated with retirement and later life. However, for time to be used well there needs to be some structure, or some pressure to act within a specific timeframe. The availability of time, but no structure to give shape to it, turns out to be a recipe for having no time at all. The scope to use one's time in a way that subverts the taken-for-granted values of our society belongs to later life. While employers can constrain our behaviour by giving us the sack, there is no such powerful constraint upon those in receipt of a pension; at least there isn't yet. The scope for taking up radical commitments is higher in the new third age than at any other stage of life. If radical action is not to one's taste, then there is scope to commit time to be alongside those who are undervalued or even despised by mainstream society, for example prisoners, those with enduring mental illness, those with severe disabilities and those at risk of deportation. Only by allowing such demands and deadlines into our lives do we find we have useful time available to us.

Norman Kember's wife pleads for his life

Pat Kember, the wife of British peace worker Dr Norman Kember who was kidnapped in Iraq, made a televised appeal on Arab TV. Speaking in a 30-second film broadcast across the Muslim world, she described her 74-year-old husband as a very caring man who believed in peace and had come to Iraq to help its people.

She declared that 'Throughout his life he bravely fought against all kinds of injustice, he went to Iraq to help the Iraqi people to stop the spread of abuse and to understand the situation in order to make Iraq a safer place. Please release Norman and his colleagues so that they can continue their work for the sake of peace in Iraq.'

The four kidnapped men, including Dr Kember, were associates of Christian Peacemaker Teams, an international NGO which promotes conflict reduction programmes in Iraq, occupied Palestine and several other places. CPT revealed prisoner abuse in Iraq well before the Abu Ghraib story became public, and its work has been widely praised by Muslims, including some leading Sunni leaders.[19]

Thomas, in making the case that elderhood involves fostering a distinctive character and orientation to life, laments how changes in modern and postmodern society have held back the development of the special capacities associated with elderhood. He comments:

'The central social and cultural challenges of our time revolve around the malignant enlargement of adulthood ... Adulthood, intoxicated by its own might, is intent on remaking (both) youth and old age in its own image...

adulthood demands that those who would remain worthy defy their age and continue to think, walk, talk, look and work like adults.'[20]

This prolonging of the middle period of the lifespan, with its emphasis on personal generativity, makes older people determined to stay young and reluctant to embrace their distinctive calling, that of *stewardship of the culture*. For Thomas, the growth in the number of older people represents an exceptionally virtuous 'windfall', because he considers older people to be the only force capable of returning our world to healthier bounds. Before judging Thomas's argument as naïve there are some aspects of his argument that should not be dismissed lightly:

- The exceptional evolutionary advantage associated with multi-generational societies raises the question as to whether this advantage is something that is limited to primitive society or whether it has relevance today.
- The narcissistic denial of ageing, to the extent that people present themselves as having all the characteristics of younger age groups, and eschew the potential capabilities associated with old age.
- The need to articulate a vision for later life other than pleasure-seeking or world weariness.

The fact that research evidence points to special developmental stages that occur in later life suggests that our style of living in later life needs to be different from that associated with middle age. There is likely to be a growth in one's interest in higher things, and a lengthening of one's moral stretch with a concern for more than just the wellbeing of oneself and one's family. Likewise there is likely to be an increase in one's ability to live with uncertainty and a sense that life and all its manifestations are interconnected. This is a description of spiritual capital. Perhaps in our fourth age we need the resource of spiritual capital to negotiate the distresses and suffering that come upon us in our fourth age. However, in the third age the challenge is to direct this spiritual capital outward, with a concern to ensure that we leave the world in a better state that we found it.

Spiritual capital

Spiritual capital is the amount of spiritual knowledge and expertise available to an individual or a culture, where spiritual is understood as the meaning, values and fundamental processes that give vitality or life to a system, whether large or small, simple or complex.[21]

Notes

1. S. Biggs (1997) 'Choosing not to be old? Mask, bodies and identity management in later life,' *Ageing and Society*, 17: 553–70.
2. W. Bridges 'January' in *Wisdom and Age* (1981) ed. J-R. Staude, Berkeley: Ross Books p.74.
3. D. A. Karp 'A decade of reminders: Changing age consciousness between fifty and sixty years old', in J. F. Grubium and J. A. Holstein, (2000) *Ageing in Everyday Life*, Oxford: Blackwell and cited by John Vincent (2003) *Old Age*, London: Routledge pp. 12–14.
4. P. Laslett (1989) *A Fresh Map of Life*, London: Weidenfeld and Nicolson
5. This stage of creating our own household and family is technically referred to as the stage of *generativity*.
6. P. Laslett (1989) op. cit. p. 2–3.
7. W. Thomas 'What is Old Age For?' www.yesmagazine.org/issues/respecting-elders-becoming-elders/1273 (viewed 23/02/2010).
8. Interestingly, Martin suggests that female whales and dolphins also live for a significant number of years after they have lost fertility, speculating

that the large sea mammals likewise have a social environment which is too complex for the young offspring to be socialized by the parenting generation alone.

9. What about the contribution of older men to the wellbeing of the little tribe of hunter gatherers? Perhaps older men carried particular wisdom? Perhaps they were the storytellers and peacemakers? They would likely have died at a younger age than women.

10. Perinatal mortality: the death of a child within the first year of life.

11. Apocryphal Gospels have Jesus writing in the sand with a stick or his finger and listing a host of sins that are likely to have beset the woman's accusers.

12. A 'cognitive process' means conscious intellectual activity, for example reasoning, thinking, remembering.

13. J. Piaget (1970/1972). 'Intellectual evolution from adolescence to adulthood', *Human Development*, 15, 1–12. p.6.

14. For an overview of Riegel's insights the following papers may be helpful: K. Riegel (1973) 'Dialectic operations: The final period of cognitive development', *Human Development*, 16, 346–370; K. Riegel (1975) 'Toward a dialectical theory of human development', *Human Development*, 18, 50–64; K. Riegel (1976) 'The dialectics of human development', *American Psychologist*, 31, 689–700; K. Riegel (1978) 'Psychology and the future', *American Psychologist*, 33, 631–647.

15. John Keats' letter to his brothers 21st December 1817, writing from Hampstead.

16. J. W. Meeker 'Wisdom and Wilderness' in *Wisdom and Age* (1981) ed. J-R. Staude; Berkley: Ross Books p.62.

17. E. H. Erikson (1964) *Insight and Responsibility*, New York: Norton p. 133.

18. E. H. Erikson, 'Identity and the Life Cycle', in *Psychological Issues*, Vol 1, No. 1 (1959) p.98.

19. From the Ekklesia website 04/12/05 (viewed 4/11/10) http://webcache. googleusercontent.com/search?q=cache:jn3zVdRYhsMJ:www.ekklesia. co.uk/content/news_syndication/article_05124patvid.shtml+baptist+o ld+hostage+Iraq+peace+activist&cd=5&hl=en&ct=clnk&gl=uk&clien t=firefox-a.

20. W. Thomas 'What is Old Age For?' in www.yesmagazine.org/issues/ respecting -elders-becoming-elders/1273 (viewed 23/02/2010).

21. Adapted from D. Zohar and I. Marshall (2005) *Spiritual Capital*, London: Bloomsbury p.41 and p.43.

CHAPTER SIX

Retirement matters

The rumour goes that it was Bismarck, the German Chancellor, who invented the 'when' of retirement. He was concerned that his army was becoming ever more feeble, as soldiers held on to their roles and status until they struggled to march on the parade ground, let alone charge into battle. Bismarck is said to have consulted his generals to ask the average age at which soldiers became infirm. The reply he received was 66 years of age, so at the age of 65 German soldiers retired. What we can be more certain about is that in 1889 Germany became the first nation in the world to adopt an old-age social insurance programme. Bismarck persuaded the German Parliament that 'those who are disabled from work by age and invalidity have a well-grounded claim to care from the state'.[1] The reason that age, rather than disability, was used as the criteria, was simply because it provided a more consistent measuring rod for the emerging state bureaucracies, and in the nineteenth century, at the age of 65, one could be pretty certain that the worker[2] would have all kinds of physical debility that would lower productivity.

Bismarck's intention was to address disability caused by age rather than to offer shelter from age itself. This linkage has ruptured over the century, which is surprising as one might assume that it would be in the interests of the state to ensure that its largesse was limited to those in clear need. This raises the spectre of collusion. Might it be that retirement benefits the employer and younger employees as much as, or even more than, the retiree? And might it be that the anticipation of thirty years of retirement carries advantages for pension funds, pension companies and the financial markets?

I am not alone in noting how the prospect of a lengthy retirement provides a great incentive to invest in retirement products. John Vincent also observes how the international pension fund market benefits hugely from scaremongering about shaky state pensions. He suggests that 'pay as you go' government-administered pensions are affordable, even in the face of the bulky baby boom generation, and they are relatively cheap to administer, as well as providing governments with a regular source of money. He argues that these clear advantages were sacrificed for the sake of the markets. By discontinuing the government run universal earnings-related pension scheme, people were forced to invest in private pension schemes which provide the major injection of new money into the markets. However, and here is the twist, the risk associated with market investments is carried by individuals rather than the pension schemes or pension funds. Vincent concludes that 'The outcome of current debates and political conflicts over securing well-funded retirement turns out to be unexpectedly critical for the future of global capitalism.'[3]

So there may be some powerful vested interests that benefit from retirement and the way it is organized. This takes us right back to the eliding of old age and disability. Liedtke, having consulted the actuarial tables for Germany going back to the days of Chancellor Otto von Bismarck, concludes:

'If the German retirement system had added as many years to the retirement age as has been added to the overall life expectancy over the past century, the official retirement age would stand at around 95 years rather than 65 years. And even if we had only tried to keep the average duration of pension payments constant over the past four decades, the retirement age for German women would today be 75 years for women and that for men 70 years.'[4]

The ease with which these calculations can be made highlight just how bizarre it is that, for more than a century, nations have persisted with a system to provide old-age security based on a meaningless measure: a person's chronological age.

Liedtke's calculation leads him to question why 'have we considered all increases in life expectancy over the past 100 years as an extension of the inactive period at the end of our life cycle?' There is a straightforward response: it is that from all angles, except for that of cost, it has advantages. Try these as a starter:

- Retirement lifts many of the workaday pressures from one's shoulders and provides scope to enjoy the benefits of cheap travel and pensioner lunches at the pub and pensioner perms at the hairdressers.
- The upcoming, younger worker can anticipate, with some accuracy, the likelihood of promotion to the jobs vacated by their retiring seniors.
- Management gains a more compliant workforce of staff, content to keep their heads down in anticipation of the future reward of stepping into the shoes of older colleagues.
- Business has a means of getting rid of those who are likely to be the highest paid, because of having accumulated service increments or long-service awards.

- Commercial companies benefit from the investment of ever-growing pension funds.
- The financial sector is energized and sustained by the movement of funds associated with 'international pension fund capitalism'.[5]

Increases in retirement age are trickling through from policy makers across Europe. However, to resolve the pension crisis by re-establishing the relationship between age and fitness to work would mean retirement age rising, not just by two or three years but by ten to fifteen years. If we really wish to ease the burden of our pensions on future generations, a more moral but less palatable response would be to scale up the level of pension contributions, with contributions increasing more significantly from the age of 50, but even so, the need to reduce pensions received over the decades of retirement would remain.

The good times rolled: The anatomy of a pension crisis

After the Second World War the proportion of people covered by the contributory state pension scheme grew rapidly, as did the value of the pensions paid out through it. These developments appeared to be costless because as the scheme expanded new contributors began to pay into it, and these people would not be drawing their pensions until the 1980s or later.

With income into the scheme rising more rapidly than the money being paid out in pensions, it seemed appropriate to pay a higher pension to retirees, even though this higher rate was greater than could be justified on the basis of actuarial assessments, or in relation to the contribution that the retirees had themselves made. The increases were justified because of the rapid economic advances of the 1950s and 60s when the standard of living was rising, so it was only fair that older, now retired workers should also benefit from the upbeat economy.

Fast forward to the 1970s and the scheme by this time had expanded to include nearly all adult workers, so the scope for additional revenue from hitherto uninsured workers disappeared. This meant additional revenue dried up, but this wasn't the only problem: larger numbers of workers were beginning to retire and expected high and rising pensions, just as they had seen for their older colleagues. However, contributions from the current workforce were no longer high enough to sustain these expanded pensions. This situation was further exacerbated by the fall in economic growth, increased levels of unemployment and an increase in the price of oil, so that by 1980 the unique historical episode, the 'golden age pensions' as the French economist Babeau[6] termed it, came to an end.[7]

In previous chapters the case has been made that those born in the 1930s and 40s, and including the baby boomers, have all been net beneficiaries of the once extensive welfare state. These are the generations that also benefit from 'golden age pensions' (although the baby boomers may be in for a shock as I suggest in Chapter One). On the basis of this largesse, especially in relation to pension entitlements, David Thomson[8] urges those born between the mid 1930s and the 1950s to moderate our claims on the state to avoid undermining the implicit contract between the generations. This implicit contract, existing between generations within a family and in society, is sutainable into the future if each generation honours its moral obligation to both the preceding and succeeding generations. We older people are at risk of being judged to have failed to honour our obligation towards the younger generation. Thomson writes:

'If the contract is broken by one generation that refuses to pay sufficiently or appropriately during their productive phase, there is then a strong incentive for succeeding generations not to invest in the contract at all and to put their faith in self-help rather than the expectations of inter-generation transfers.'[9]

Thomson continues:

'what societies must and will find themselves discussing is why the younger adults today can be expected to play the part assigned to them by history, that of willing funders of a lifetime welfare state, which they themselves will never inhabit. Upon a resolution of this hinge all questions concerning the elderly.'[10]

Thomson, in alerting policy makers to the 'ruinous implication' of the mounting unfairness between the generations, is more a prophet than a rabble-rouser seeking to set one generation against another. He not only warns of the looming crisis, he suggests a starting point from which to pick our way through the predicament. Thomson, like me, was born in 1953, and he proposes that our generation should offer itself as a 'sacrifice generation' on which to pivot a reversion to resourcing younger generations. There are some reasons why those born in the early fifties might be better placed than other age cohorts to be the 'turn around generation'. The motivation might be there because it eases the pressure on 'our' offspring, rather than a more distant age cohort, and we are a generation that has had most of the things that money can buy. Now what we want more than anything is to declutter our lives. Perhaps I should speak for myself here.

A 'pivot' generation?

The moral case for accepting the role of 'pivot', or the turn around generation is strong:

- It acknowledges the additional financial strain that younger age cohorts will have to shoulder as a result of the bank bailouts and the long term increase in national debt.
- It acknowledges that the demographics, specific to Britain, are changing. With more babies being born, this adds further to the tax burden on younger generations as they pay tax for schools, etc., as well as for health services and pensions for older generations, and to bring up their families.
- Those born in the 1940s and 50s have benefited from the development of educational and career opportunities, as well as steady increases in other aspects of the quality of life, not to mention the ever-growing increase in the value of property. This compares with younger age cohorts who face far less opportunity in relation to these 'social goods', as well as the disappointment linked with the inevitable 'diminishing marginal utility' of goods (described in Chapter Four).
- There is recognition that public policy will almost always be slanted in favour of older generations, because of the voting power of the over–50s. After the age of 50 everyone can envisage themselves benefiting from the status quo within a relatively short period of time, while

support for youth-focused policies is necessarily much more transitory, and young voters are often unaware of where their interests lie.

- For the last decade, pensioners have been significantly less likely to have been part of a low-income household than those of working age.

The possibility of being the 'turn around' generation may not appeal to those who have already opted for the 'everyone for themselves from birth to death' principle. However, Christians must think seriously about taking on this mantle. Christian commitment to justice and to the flourishing of the Creation means that the challenge for Christians is not whether to be part of a pivot generation, but *how to* play a part in the turn around.

The assumed solution to re-balancing fairness between the generations is to extend the retirement age upwards, and many governments have chosen to do this. While this may ease the tax burden, it is unlikely to help younger people achieve the 'narrative of identity'[11] that comes from decent employment. With both men *and* women now seeking paid employment, unless the amount of paid work increases substantially, raising the retirement age is likely to *add* to the existing difficulty of younger people getting a good job. Increasing the age of retirement is the least imaginative way through the problem of intergenerational fairness, because it increases the likelihood of my generation staying on the top rungs of the ladder and receiving 'top dollar' remuneration for even longer and may even add to the tensions between generations.

There are more imaginative, work-related responses that would enable my generation to 'pivot', and act generously, to relieve pressure on the squeezed younger generations. The work that needs to be done in our society is significantly greater than what is expressed in the labour market. There is work that gets done for which money is never paid. Women are particularly familiar with this, as child-rearing and housework are major examples of vital work[12] that takes place outside the remunerated labour market. One of the ever present examples of unpaid but vital labour that my generation undertakes is care for grandchildren, and care for their own parents who are likely to be in or on the cusp of their fourth age. The challenge or pivot point for my generation is whether we are able and willing to act in a way that strengthens this realm of unpaid, often unacknowledged, but nonetheless essential work. This theme is taken up by the World Health Organization in the promotion of 'Healthy Cities'. This could be described as a new wave of public health that harnesses the contributions of ordinary people alongside professional workers. Allan Kellehear develops this idea to include widening the involvement of ordinary people in end of life care.[13] What is not being described or encouraged is 'job substitution', where a volunteer takes on the role of paid worker.

Kellehear uses the word 'compassion' in a very precise way, emphasising 'being with' and providing a tender response to the distress and suffering of others. Therefore a compassionate approach involves *partnership with each other* as vulnerable human beings. This he suggests could form a third wave[14] of public health, which would:

'Emphasize inclusiveness based on universal human experience of suffering and well-being, and not simply categories of 'illness', 'disease' or health state. The idea of compassion is able to transcend and render irrelevant the old twentieth-century categories of 'health' and 'welfare'.[15]

The growth of professional and 'paid for' care has narrowed the scope for partnership in relation to the universal struggles that everyone has to negotiate, especially those struggles that come with late old age and the approach of death. On one level, what is proposed by Kellehear may seem to be just an extension of voluntary work and voluntary organization, but it is more than this: it offers a theoretical foundation for widening the part that ordinary people can play in relation to health and wellbeing. In particular, it asks professional workers to allow others (us) to contribute. It asks us to step out of the mindset of the 'contaminating other' – those who 'have a problem', compared with the 'us' who are in some way 'pure'; and it encourages us all to draw on our experiences of loss and death, and from this experience to support those currently assailed.

Kellehear seeks to make the 'partnership' that is the essence of compassion the first priority for a fresh expression of public health. The steps he outlines to bring about this new approach widen the repertoire of unpaid work. In particular it gives volunteers more to do than run hospital shops, and fundraise for scanners and other items that are then managed directly by health care professionals.

Work for free – or be miserable for a very long time!

Although the economy in Britain may have grown over the last twenty-five years, research indicates that there has been little improvement in the quality of our social relationships and social wellbeing. In fact the opposite has happened: there have been significant increases in loneliness, isolation and disconnectedness – issues that Kellehear would wish to include in the third wave of public health. It is estimated that in Britain today seven million people experience severe lack of connection with others and a further one million report that they have no-one to turn to if they are in trouble, or no-one who appreciates them.[16] We may have become wealthier but we have become more sad and lonely, and, given our potentially long lives, we shall have to endure this state for many long decades unless we take steps to ameliorate our condition.

This prospect of being miserable for three decades or more should provide an additional incentive to the 'never had it so good' generation to be a pivot on which the direction of advantage can turn. In order to counter this potential for sadness and loneliness among older people, work activity needs to stay in the frame. The imaginative or oblique way in which this is possible, without disadvantaging younger generations, is to *donate* our capacity for work. For example, there is the work of providing a monthly mini-bus trip for those on the cusp of their fourth age. There is the work of contributing to the University of the Third Age, there is the work of coaching young people in a sport, there is the work of supporting those seeking asylum in Britain. There is work with prisoners and ex-prisoners. For those who wish to combine prayerfulness with action there is SPEAK, which combines campaigning and praying in relation to global issues. This list could be enormous, and all the items on such a list would involve *work*, and psychologists are now alert to the capacity of donated work to elicit positive emotions that counter some of the physiological and psychological hazards of later life.

In reviewing our lives, many of the hassles and troubles are likely to have been work-related. Whether it is the dishonest colleague or the bullying boss, there can be few who have been spared sleepless nights because of the negative emotions triggered by our employment. Psychologists have now discovered how negative emotions such as these take their toll on us. Negative emotions such as fear, anger or disgust prepare us mentally and physically for immediate action against an object or situation that poses a threat. In contrast, positive emotions such as joy, hope, optimism, love, contentment and gratitude energize us for positive action, creating a virtuous, life-enhancing upwards spiral. There is a simple question that follows from this: Where and how are we most likely to be party to positive emotions rather than negative emotions? Is it most likely to be through involvement in paid work or by donating our capacity for work?

Barbara Fredrickson has studied the impact of positive emotions on our physical and mental wellbeing. Her research highlights the capacity of positive emotions to undo the cardiovascular effects of negative emotions. It is known that when we experience stress our heart rate increases, so too does our blood sugar level and our immune system goes into overdrive – basically, when we are stressed our physiology is gearing up for action. If we remain stressed long term this can lead to chronic conditions, especially coronary disease. Both laboratory research and surveys show that positive emotions – such as joy, playfulness, enjoyment – help us to relax back from stress to a normal physiological state.[17] Fredrickson calls this the '*undoing effect*' of positive emotions.

There is a further aspect to Fredrickson's work: the capacity of positive emotions to encourage venturesomeness. To use the language of psychology, positive emotions broaden our behavioural repertoire by encouraging novel, varied and exploratory thoughts and actions, which over time widen a person's skills and resourcefulness. At first glance this is common sense, in that if we have a good experience we are more likely to come back for more. But when put alongside the physiological impact of negative emotions, the importance of donated labour, and its greater capacity to generate positive emotions, then *the value of donated work to the donor rises significantly.* The extension of paid employment for more and more years of our lives, i.e. raising the age of retirement, potentially generates negative emotions such as anxiety, annoyance, resentment and so on, which, as well as being stressors, narrow our perspective and undermine creativity and inventiveness. This is not a recommended way in which to grow old.

The Greek word *eudaimonia* is used to describe that extraordinarily positive state of mind when moral or virtuous behaviour coincides with happiness. Research into this exceptionally positive experience has been undertaken by Jonathan Haidt. He uses the term 'elevation' to describe the almost physical response we can have to the remarkable moral behaviour of others, and although it is not an unpleasant emotion, it often *moves us to tears.* But more than this, Haidt shows how this experience motivates us to act more virtuously ourselves, making us feel lifted up and optimistic about the human enterprise.[18]

I recall having an experience like this when I was involved in some research for the Church of Scotland, which involved meeting with people who lived in some of the toughest housing schemes. The discussion turned to the subject of drug addiction and the role of methadone. I noted comments such as 'Methadone is nae answer. It's just about getting addicts off the back of the Social Services and doctors'. And 'There's no effort being made to help people get their lives back. They are walking about like zombies, just going to get their prescription and then going back to have a sleep.' I asked the group whether they could see any ways in which they could help those who were on methadone. People thought for a while and one suggestion was that singing might help. So perhaps the church could run some singing groups? I suggested. This was thought about and discussed and abandoned because those in the group knew that methadone would make it unlikely that they would find the energy or motivation to turn up. This reality was reflected on and someone said, 'Aye, but we could go to them and sing with them in their wee flats.'

Interestingly, this vignette that is so special to me (and probably would be special to Kellehear as an excellent illustration of the potential third wave of public health), involves donated labour, but it also involves hard-won insight, rooted imagination and courage – and it was to be a gift. Haidt suggests that elevation combines warm, open feelings with motivation to act more virtuously, making us feel lifted up and optimistic about the human enterprise. This was the effect this group had on me, and what I describe as a virtuous upward spiral. There is no means of placing an economic value on such a positive dynamic, and I suggest that it could only have been triggered by the generosity of spirit of those willing to give of their exceptional compassion.

Acting as a 'pivot'

Our efforts to act as a 'pivot' generation could be helped by changes in the structure of employment. We currently think in terms of full- or part-time employment, but there are potential gains from restructuring employment into groupings of 12 hours, which could be spread over a week or even, as nurses often do, undertaken as a single shift. Reshaping employment contracts in this way would facilitate greater flexibility to downscale and upscale. For example, a couple might choose to undertake four employment 'batches', so they would undertake 48 hours work. This might involve contracts of employment with up to four employers, or perhaps three twelve hour batches (36 hours) with just a single employer. It may be that one of them takes on just a single 12-hour contract whilst the other has three 12-hour contracts. This flexibility would be welcomed by older and young people both of whom might opt to undertake a single twelve hour batch of employment. For older people this could bring some continuity of employment rather than having to cope with the stern transition from full-time employment to the no-employment of retirement. For young people it would give scope to engage with further or higher education as well as demonstrate their prowess to employers. It would also enable us to taste the reality that we need far less income than we realize to live a fulfilled life.[19]

Reassessing the work/life balance is essential in the third age, especially if one senses that there are distinctive tasks to take on as we get older. If our view of successful ageing is restricted to the maintenance of a midlife pattern of activity for as long as we can, a more contemplative approach to ageing can be missed. The contemplative potential of ageing enables greater indwelling and considering, as well as increased interiority. With this comes the scope to redefine 'self', our relationship to others, and to engage with of some of the existential questions that relate to life and death. This more spiritual or 'mindful' approach to later life requires time and space, and that means limiting the extent of work, whether remunerated or donated. Bishop describes mindfulness or spirituality as 'a kind of non-elaborative, non-judgmental, present-centred awareness in which each thought, feeling or sensation that arises in the attentional field is acknowledged and accepted as it is'.[20] According to Bishop and his colleagues there are two aspects to mindfulness. The first aspect:

'involves the self-regulation of attention so that it is maintained on immediate experience, thereby allowing for increased recognition of mental events in the present moment'.[21]

The second aspect,

'involves adopting a particular orientation toward one's experiences in the present moment, an orientation that is characterized by curiosity, openness, and acceptance'.[22]

Mindfulness, with its strong resemblance to the formal spiritual practices on the world's religions, provides a pulse beat that creates and sustains a virtuous upward spiral. Brown and his team researched the relationship between spirituality or mindfulness and financial desire and wellbeing. They found that the larger the gap between financial desires and financial reality then the lower a person's subjective wellbeing was likely to be, but note this: the accumulation of wealth did not tend to close the gap between what people had and what people wanted. If ever there was a treadmill this is surely it. For those for whom 'mindfulness' was a regular part of their lives, there was a significantly lower financial-desire discrepancy and therefore higher subjective well-being. From this research Brown and his colleagues conclude that mindfulness is linked with a sense of 'having enough'.[23]

Go to church each week – it's easier than working twice as hard!

American researchers suggest that going to church once a week improves people's wellbeing equivalent to their salary being doubled.[24]

If there is to be a 'pivot' generation, then the ability to say 'enough' and to feel deeply and assuredly that one has 'enough' is critical. To let go of actual and potential advantage is only possible if we feel secure, both practically and emotionally, that we have 'enough'. To achieve this state we need to ensure that we educate our soul and enrich our inner lives so as to simplify our outer lives. This focus on interiority is not a description of disengagement, although as a result the business of 'having and getting' may lose it's attraction; rather it is what Erikson refers to as 'durable hope'.[25] This state of durable hope is the driver of the necessary resilience to cope with the hits that we take in later life, but more than this, the state of durable hope may also bring out the best in us.

Notes

1. American Social Security Administration see http://www.socialsecurity.gov/history/age65.html.
2. To keep the record straight, according to the American Social Security Administration, 'Germany initially set age 70 as the retirement age (and Bismarck himself was 74 at the time) and it was not until 27 years later (in 1916) that the age was lowered to 65. By that time, Bismarck had been dead for 18 years.' http://www.socialsecurity.gov/history/age65.html.
3. J. Vincent (2003) *Old Age*; London: Routledge p. 80.
4. P. M. Liedtke, 12 February 2006, European Papers on the new welfare;

'From Bismarck's Pension Trap to the new Silver Workers' Paper No.4 / 2006 Published by The Risk Institute http://eng.newwelfare. org/2006/02/12/from-bismarck%e2%80%99s-pension-trap-to-the-new-silver-workers-of-tomorrow-reflections-on-the-german-pension-problem/.

5. This is a term used by John Vincent (2003) op. cit. p. 80.
6. See A. Babeau (1985) *La fin des retraites?* Paris: Hachette.
7. Adapted from P. Johnson, C. Conrad and D. Thomson (eds) (1989) *Workers versus Pensioners*, London: Centre for Economic Policy Research p.14.
8. See D. Thomson (1996) *Selfish Generations? How Welfare States Grow Old*, Cambridge: The White Horse Press.
9. P. Johnson, C. Conrad and D. Thomson (eds) (1989) op. cit. p.6.
10. D. Thomson 'The Welfare State and Generation Conflict' in P. Johnson, C. Conrad and D. Thomson (eds) (1989) op.cit. p.54.
11. The significance of achieving a positive narrative of identity is essential to achieving appropriate and healthy self-esteem. This idea is at the heart of Richard Sennet's 'The Corrosion of Character' which has the sub-title 'The personal consequences of work in the New Capitalism'. See R. Sennet (1998) *The Corrosion of Character*, New York: W. W. Norton and Co.
12. There is clear evidence for the value of housework and homemaking by the effect it has on longevity: being married adds years to men's lives, but for women, it takes years away.
13. See A. Kellehear (2005) *Compassionate Cities*, London: Routledge.
14. The first wave of public health: clean drinking water, better sewage systems, building regulations and control of infectious diseases; The second wave of public health: health education, legislation and control around unhealthy lifestyles.
15. Kellehear (2005) op.cit. p161.
16. See The Young Foundation (2009) *Sinking and Swimming: understanding Britain's unmet needs*, London: The Young Foundation.
17. B. L. Fredrickson, R. A. Mancuso, C. Branigan, and M. M. Tugade (2000) 'The undoing effect of positive emotions'; Motivation and Emotion 24, 237–258.
18. J. Haidt (2003) 'Elevation and the positive psychology of morality'; in C. Keyes and J. Haidt (eds), *Flourishing: Positive psychology and the life well-lived*, Washington, D. C.: American Psychological Association.
19. The New Economics Foundation makes the case for a 21-hour working week – see A. Coote, A. Simms and J. Franklin (2010) *21 hours,*

London: New Economics Foundation http://www.neweconomics.org/publications/21-hours. I suggest that my proposal allows more flexibility and greater choice.

20. S. R. Bishop, M. Lau, S. Shapiro, and L. Carlson (2004) 'Mindfulness: A Proposed Operational Definition', *Clinical Psychology: Science and Practice* 11:230–241. p.232.
21. Ibid. p.232.
22. Ibid p.232.
23. K. W. Brown (2009) 'When what one has is enough: Mindfulness, financial desire discrepancy, and subjective well being', *Journal of Research in Personality*, 43(5).
24. Cited in 'Life Satisfaction: The State of Knowledge and Implications for Government' pub. by the Prime Minister's Strategy Unit Dec. 2002 See http://webarchive.nationalarchives.gov.uk/20060715135117/http://strategy.gov.uk/seminars/life_satisfaction/index.asp.
25. E. Erikson (1982) *The Life Cycle Completed*, New York: Norton p.62.

CHAPTER SEVEN

Inheritance matters

The question of inheritance has been around since the beginning of history, and different cultures and religious groups have surrounded the practice with different rules. Islam, more than any religion, has established procedures to ensure clarity and a degree of fairness, as well as charitable giving from the deceased's estate. At the beginning of the Old Testament, or the Torah to use the Jewish name, the basic rules in relation to inheritance are spelt out in Numbers, the law book compiled by Moses as he led the Children of Israel through the wilderness. Moses determined that:

'If a man dies and leaves no son, give his inheritance to his daughters. If he has no daughter, give his inheritance to his brothers. If he has no brothers, give his inheritance to his father's brothers. If his father had no brothers, give his inheritance to the nearest relative in this clan, that he may possess it.'[1]

While there are plenty of references to inheritance in the Old Testament, and the antics that go on to make sure one is first in line to benefit from a dying father's blessing,[2] there is scarcely any reference to the inheritance of material goods and wealth in the New Testament. The only reference is made by St Paul in the second of his letters to the Christians in Corinth. Here, almost as an aside, in the midst of preparing the Corinthian Christians for his third visit, assuring them that he will not be a burden to them, he comments, 'After all, children should not have to save up for their parents, but parents for their children.'[3] This aphorism-like commendation of inheritance is one of the few direct references in the Gospels to the responsibility across generations. Walter Brueggemann comments that, especially in matters to do with age and family practice, the Bible often 'appropriates and practises what is common in ancient Near Eastern culture, and it likely does so without great intentionality or reflectiveness.'[4] Brueggemann would probably agree that this comment by St Paul, made *en passant*, seems scarcely intentional in theological terms.

In the absence of any explicit teaching on inheritance in the Gospels, we have to deduce the counsel that would be forthcoming from Jesus. This approach is one that we are familiar with in relation to most of the contemporary ethical issues that were inconceivable in the time of Jesus. So for counsel in relation to inheritance, the foremost themes would be:

- Jesus urging us not to worry about material things
- Jesus representing the generosity of God
- Jesus taking the side of the disparaged and excluded

These aspects of the way Jesus lived and taught combine to give clear guidance for Christians regarding our approach to inheritance. The desire to accumulate wealth on earth is likely to be wrong-headed; the desire to keep assets within the family is equally likely to be wrong-headed, and our actions are to emulate the essential generosity that is at the heart of God. So, sorry St Paul, cultural aphorisms that encourage the gathering of resources through one's life, so that they can be passed on to the next generation, will not pass muster.

Jesus frequently suggests that those who follow him will be inheritors of the Kingdom of God. Better theologians than I have struggled to work out what this means, and so it is with some trepidation that I offer my interpretation. In following Jesus we receive all that really matters in life, and we receive these things in abundance and without end. Sometimes this is referred to as salvation, or redemption, to emphasize the possibility of living a life set free from the dastardliness of self-interest and the turbulence of our psyche. In its positive aspects, becoming an inheritor of the Kingdom of God, through following Jesus, includes being blessed in a sense of security and continuity, precisely calming the fears associated with the unknowns that surround our experience of later life.

It is bad form that so little attention is given to this issue of inheritance, either in our churches or in public debate, because inheritance, in the material sense, ploughs straight into the dastardliness of self-interest and emotional turbulence. Although inheritance might be little talked about, it is much thought about. Having wealth to pass on after one's death can be like a weapon to wield to bring mayhem among those who gather to hear the reading of a last will and testament. In the past it would have been a minority of people who would have benefited from someone's estate. But as household wealth has increased, particularly wealth represented by house ownership, so too has the frequency of inheritance.

Cheap status

One of the easiest ways of getting people to hold you in high esteem is through wealth, and this cheap route to esteem may be one of the reasons why some of the wealthiest people have shown themselves reluctant to pass their wealth down the generations, preferring to give the bulk to charitable foundations. Too much wealth, or even the promise of wealth, can cause havoc for the offspring. As the adage goes, it is possible to choke on a silver spoon. The film *Born Rich* focuses on the risk of drug abuse, the disincentive to work and the perpetual fear of disinheritance that can pervade the lives of children of wealthy parents. However, for most people, if we ourselves are beneficiaries of the wealth accumulated by a previous generation, its relative modesty may bring some financial ease to our lives rather than cause an existential crisis.

There is very little UK research into the way wealth gets passed down through the generations, and what there is shows some surprising results. David Willetts notes the research undertaken by Chris Hammet (sic)[5] into the 'estates' people leave behind when they die. The straightforward assumption would be that as more and more people buy their homes, this would mean there would be an increase in the number of houses that are inherited by the next generation. However, the number of houses being inherited is significantly smaller than the growth in house ownership among the oldest generation. This suggests one of two things: either that our houses have become collateral needed to support a very long old age; or secondly, the bumper sticker 'Spending the kids' inheritance' is being taken more seriously than has been realized. Both, of course, may be true.

A generation denied the right to buy

'Millions of young people are being forced to abandon their hopes of buying a home ... Rises in house prices, coupled with lenders demanding bigger deposits, is turning Britain into a nation of renters. Worst hit are the 'in-betweeners' – low income workers who are unlikely to be offered social housing, but cannot afford to purchase a home of their own.'

The Chartered Institute of Housing says that 'House ownership is out of reach of a lot of people ... The golden age of home ownership is coming to an end. The CIH says in the most expensive parts of the country, first-time buyers need to stump up deposits of more than £40,000 to get on the property ladder.

In Germany, almost half the population rent because there are more renting options and standards are higher. That compares with 34.5 per cent of the population in France living in rented accommodation, 32.2 per cent in Holland and 26.7 per cent in the UK.'[6]

It is clear that more people than ever before benefit from inheritance, but it would seem that the largesse from one's elders may not turn out to be as generous as had been anticipated. One group in the population seems to do disproportionately well out of inheritance. Rumour has it that the category of people who are often the wealthiest in western societies are elderly widows and elderly spinsters who easily outlive their menfolk and gather up their inheritance. However, the biggest threat to this accumulated wealth is the cost of residential care. Although the cost of nursing may be met from public money, the remaining costs have to be met from one's assets, including one's house. The power of this policy to provoke resentment is immense, and that is one of the problems with inheritance: its anticipation incites a host of complex and unseemly anxieties, as well as sentiments that are too shameful to be voiced except by the most hard-faced.

Mostly we inherit at the stage in our lifespan when we least need the money. However, for families with money to spare there is scope to address this. This way of transferring wealth between the generations is referred to as *inter vivos transfers* and involves gifts from the living. These wealth transfers often happen at key junctions in life, for example going to college, getting married, setting up home, on the birth of a child and so on. As well as noting the significance of money, stocks and shares, property, antiques and all the kinds of things that get passed from the older generation to the younger, Bourdieu, the French sociologist, also highlights the significance of *cultural capital*. The essence of cultural capital is self-assurance; it is a form of confidence. It includes knowledge about how to manage oneself in all manner of circumstances, the social graces that come from going to a good school, that come from having parents who have demonstrably negotiated the hazards of life and achieved more than a modicum of success. Often economic inheritance, including *inter vivos transfers,* and the disposition towards self-assurance coalesce, and this gives exceptional advantage to those so blest.

Fragile households

As well as impacting on individuals, inheritance, both economic and cultural, has a societal impact: it increases the gap between rich and poor and creates a cycle of privilege, and a cycle of exclusion. Inheritance has always had this effect, but the situation has intensified as more people now benefit from inheritance and become well placed to continue the pattern. It would be wrong to try and legislate against or talk down the efforts of families to 'straighten the way' for younger family members. But even when shored up by inheritance, the self-sufficiency of the family has come under pressure due to:

- smaller family size and an increase in childlessness
- the expectation that the younger generation will leave home[7] and probably never return
- the increasing rate of divorce
- the increasing number of people living in single person households.

The fragility of our families is not just a problem for public policy, it is a 'here now' problem for each and every one of us. Traditionally we rely on family members when we are in need, whether those needs be emotional, financial or practical. So when our families become more fragile we too are likely to feel more vulnerable. As well as relying on our family for inheritance, both financial and cultural, we also look to our families for shelter, food, play, conversation, sleeping securely and pooling economic resources. These are the essential resources for everyday life. Small families face a lot of pressure to provide these essentials simply because there are fewer people to provide them. With just Mum and Dad, or maybe just a single parent, the tasks of earning, driving, cooking, cleaning and caring for the young and the sick all have to be done. The stress and strain of carrying out the everyday tasks at the heart of family life may have become so onerous that a tipping point has been reached, so the precariousness of the single life has become preferable to the hard work and emotional intensity of family life.

The Widow of Nain

Soon afterwards, Jesus went to a town called Nain, and his disciples and a large crowd went along with him. As he approached the town gate, a dead person was being carried out – the only son of his mother, and she was a widow. And a large crowd from the town was with her. When the Lord saw her, his heart went out to her and he said, 'Don't cry.' Then he went up and touched the coffin, and those carrying it stood still. He said, 'Young man, I say to you, get up!' The dead man sat up and began to talk, and Jesus gave him back to his mother.

Luke, chapter 7 vv. 11 – 15 (NIV)

Older women, often those in deep old age, are likely to find themselves living alone precisely at the time when their vulnerability is highest. One of the growing consequences is the risk older people face, and older women in particular, of being *groomed* by those who seek to take advantage. This, of course, is a hazard that is particularly related to having a lot of money. With the absence of close family, and friends who may also have become old, the isolation of older people means that those with complex and perhaps underhand intentions can insinuate their way into the life of those who are at the stage of relinquishing their prowess. I mention this distressing issue for two reasons. The first reason is to *name it*. The grooming of older people is increasing and it is wise to be more alert to it. The second reason why I refer to it is to illustrate what I have chosen to refer to in earlier chapters as dastardliness.

Dastardliness is a four-syllable word that I use instead of a single syllable word: sin. When sin gets mentioned it turns people off, whereas when the word 'dastardly' is used people prick up their ears and attend. Grooming older people is a dastardly act. It is dastardly because it involves trickery aimed at taking advantage of another: grooming behaviour gets masked behind a close and helping relationship, which clearly benefits and reassures the vulnerable person. There is a second aspect to the dastardliness of this issue: the fact of drawing attention to the prevalence of the grooming of older people adds to the inclination of older people to be suspicious of relationships across the generations and in relation to friendship in general. Dastardliness, just like sin, creates a downward negative spiral. Often, dastardliness has its roots in a misuse of power and the taking advantage of others, but our need to act in this way is likely to be a product of the dastardliness that has been perpetrated on the offender. Dastardliness is contagious; it runs deep within us all, and trying to limit the impact of dastardliness costs a great deal both at a personal and a public level.

In Japan there is a social mechanism that gives the older person some control in relation to those who accompany them through late old age, and who will inherit their wealth and give continuity to the family name. It is *yōshi engumi* or adult adoption. This secures family support for the elderly in return for the offer of inheritance, and more even than this, family lineage is continued through the adopted adult son and his existing family. It is a process that re-balances power and therefore lessens the possibility of the dastardly grooming of older people. Akiko Hashimoto describes how this process works in Japan:

'As a childless couple, the Yamadas' plan for this old-age security began years ago in their middle age, when they turned to this traditional Japanese option (of *yōshi engumi*). (They) have now invested almost all their savings in their adopted son, consciously grooming him and his wife as their future caregivers, which is for them the most important part of the "understanding"... Most of the financial transfer from the older to the younger generation seems to have taken place already: the Yamadas have made the down payment for their adopted son's house while they themselves continue to live in a small rental unit. As such, their adaptation to old age, and Shizu preparing for the likelihood of widowhood, has been deliberately planned. She has intentionally created an extended family where none existed, and has even concocted a live-in surrogate grandchild, Toto-chan. Through the series of steps she has taken over the past 15 years she has consciously made herself a future beneficiary of this family support system.' [8]

This Japanese approach is described to indicate the scope for different approaches to managing the earning, driving, cooking, cleaning and caring for the young, the sick and very old, which are the standard tasks of any household. One hopes that we are at the beginning of a host of innovations in relation to the 'household', because the current model is in rapid decline. The increasing number of single-person households, of which many are older people living alone, does not bode well for the future. Single-person households are financially costly to the individual and to the environment, and the risk of loneliness and its capacity to disrupt personal equanimity runs high.

The high level of mobility that we have become used to can easily undermine friendships and neighbourliness. It can take a long time to foster this aspect of cultural or social capital. Often it is only when we are older that we begin truly to appreciate friendship and neighbourliness, neither of which can be created in a rush or to order. When we grow old, gerontologists talk of our need for triangulation of support: relatives, friends and neighbours. However, relatives have come to be in short supply for most people, as a consequence of the steady move towards small families. I note how my mother, as the youngest of twelve, provided regular support for older siblings who had remained in the neighbourhood. Now we may have one or two or maybe no siblings, so the frailness of families, combined with high levels of geographic mobility, undermine our need for a 'triangulation of support'.

As well as geographic mobility and the norm of small families, the impact of divorce has to be factored in. We know that children often take a big hit from the divorce of their parents, but what is less acknowledged are the consequences of divorce as we get older. Divorce can confuse the pattern of obligation and responsibility in a family, and it is something that can have a particular impact on older men. After a divorce the likelihood is that the children live with their mother and the relationship with their father can be strained or distant. His children's loyalty is likely to be to their mother rather than to him, and should a serious illness or other misfortune befall him, the chances are that he will have to negotiate his future relying on his own resources rather than the care and compassion of his children.

Friendship matters

In our long old age, and in a context where family support is likely to be patchy, skills for building and keeping friendships are essential. Families are not the only source of support and tenderness, but making friends is largely learned behaviour. Our capacity for friendship is part of the cultural inheritance that we get from our upbringing and family of origin, and its value has increased substantially. However, the value of friendship can be annulled by pressure to move when we retire. An easy-care flat with sea views can be seductive and far more tempting than old friends, and the assumption that it will be easy to keep in touch can give reassurance that nothing will be lost. Except that it will be lost. Longstanding friendships that enable 'popping-in' i.e. seeing friends on most days, have been shown to be deeply significant to the wellbeing of older people.

FRIENDSHIP MORE CONDUCIVE TO HAPPINESS THAN MONEY

Friendships are more important than money when it comes to happiness, according to new research from the Institute of Education. An increase in seeing friends and relatives from 'once or twice a month' to 'on most days' brings as much happiness as an extra £85,000 a year added to the pay packet. And talking to our neighbours more often can be worth an additional £37,000 of happiness a year, finds the research, based on data from the British Household Panel Survey. On the other hand, a decrease in the amount of face-to-face contact with friends and relatives from 'on most days' to 'once or twice a week' brings an increase in unhappiness worth £15,500 a year.

Dr. Nattavudh Powdthavee, who carried out the research, says: 'This shows that non-economic factors such as having active social relationships can make a strong difference to our happiness. One potential explanation is that social activities tend to require our attention while they are being experienced, so that the joy derived from them lasts longer in our memory. Income, on the other hand, is mostly in the background. We don't normally have to pay so much

---

attention to the fact that we'll be getting a pay packet at the end of the week or month. So the joy derived from income probably doesn't last as long.' [9]

Okinawa is a region of Japan which is home to the longest-living people in the world. The much-studied people here have the lowest incidence of heart disease, cancer and dementia, despite the fact that Okinawa is the poorest area of Japan. Much research has focused on diet as the chief contributor to Okinawans' healthy old age, as well as the discipline of *hara hachi-bu* 'eating until you are 80 per cent full.' However, friendship of the 'popping-in' style also prevails. *Yuimaru* is Okinawan dialect for warm-hearted and friendly cooperative effort. *Yuimaru* means a commitment to taking care of each other, and so elderly single women will share vegetables from their gardens; at meal times each will bring a dish to eat together and they contribute to a community fund that can help those with particular needs. This may be another aspect of the Okinawans' longevity secret.

It is possible to work consciously to create cultural capital. For example, the Older Women's CoHousing project began in London in 1998 based on a Danish model to support active and healthy ageing. The project involves securing housing close to each other, with each person (usually women who live alone) having their own front doors, but able to offer each other mutual support as they get older. The project also aims to adopt energy efficiency and to be a resource for the local community. Members of the OWCH project describe themselves:

'We are a group of twenty or so women, almost all of whom live alone. We come from a variety of backgrounds and cultures and our ages range from the mid-fifties to around eighty. Although we are all very different and have our own particular interests, family connections, work – some of us are still working – or health difficulties or disabilities, what we all share is a determination to stay as self-dependent and active as we can as we get older.'[10]

In hard times, the traditional response has always been to hold more things in common. Both in the USA and in the UK there has been a surge in the number of Christian groups being formed essentially to reclaim a simpler and less pressured life. Commentators such as Tom Sine suggest that: 'The global recession is a Kairos moment. We have an opportunity to reduce our economic vulnerability, in order to increase our availability, time and resource, to become God's compassion to our neighbours, near and far.'[11] The Northumbria Community was one of the first new expressions of monasticism in the UK, beginning in the late 1970s. The Northumbria Community describe their life together as combining prayer, availability and vulnerability and they draw encouragement from Bonhoeffer, when writing to his brother:

'The renewal of the church will come from a new type of monasticism which only has in common with the old an uncompromising allegiance to the Sermon on the Mount. It is high time men and women banded together to do this.'[12]

The Northumbria Community is committed to 'enacting a fearful hope for society.' In various parts of the UK, groups of people meet together, usually once a month, as local expressions of the Northumbria Community. Most groups meet in someone's house. All are ecumenical in nature and exercise some form of hospitality. Generally there is some kind of liturgy shared at some point in the time together; most frequently this is an Evening Office.[13] The Northumbria Community also takes comfort from the writing of Rudolph Bahro, an early eco-activist based in East Germany:

'When the forms of an old culture are dying, the new culture is created by a few people who are not afraid to be insecure.'[14]

This observation from Bahro is relevant to the challenge of being a 'pivot' generation committed to achieving fairness between the generations. The pattern of entitlements rooted in a one-off economic boom belongs to a culture that is dying. The creation of a new culture, Bahro advises, is best done by those who are not afraid to be insecure. From what we know of the lifespan, it is likely to be older people who have conquered insecurities and it is the older generation that has to ask future generations to create a more gentle way of living than they themselves have been able to achieve. It is for older people to imagine and experiment with alternatives, in order to provide a healthier cultural inheritance for future generations, and this takes us to the crux of what it is to be a 'pivot' generation.

Notes

1. Numbers 27 vv.8–11 (NIV).
2. I am thinking here of Esau and Jacob, but I could equally be thinking of Tamar's ploy to catch out Judah.
3. 2 Corinthians 12 v. 14 (NIV).
4. Walter Brueggemann (Editor's Foreword) in *Biblical Perspectives on Aging* by J. G. Harris (1987) Philadelphia: Fortress Press p. x.

5. The reference made by Willetts should be to Prof. Chris Hamnett, Professor of Geography at Kings College London and previously with the Open University.

6. Based on a report by Anne Campbell in the *Metro* August 16 2010.

7. In the UK there is a growing number of two-generation households consisting of parent(s) and unmarried or unsettled grown-up children.

8. A. Hashimoto (1996) *The Gift of Generations*, Cambridge: Cambridge University Press p.4–5.

9. Press Release 30 April 2007 relating to the work of Dr Nattavudh Powdthavee, a research officer in the Centre for the Economics of Education at the Institute of Education. *Metro*: 1 May 2007. This research was published in the Journal of Socio Economics, 37(4), 1459–1480 "Putting a Price Tag on Friends, Relatives, and Neighbours: Using Surveys of Life-Satisfaction to Value Social Relationships."

10. See http://www.owch.org.uk/index.html.

11. B. Draper 'Like the Early Christians', the *Church Times* 27 August 2010 p.15.

12. Dietrich Bonhoeffer, in a letter to his brother; a more detailed reference is not provided on the website of the Northumbria Community

13. Adapted from the website of the Northumbria Community http://www.northumbriacommunity.org/who-we-are.

14. This quotation is not referenced on the website of the Northumbria Community http://www.northumbriacommunity.org/

CHAPTER EIGHT

An epidemic of narcissism?

In choosing to forgo self-interest, it is wise to be confident of your assessment of the situation. In encouraging my generation, the baby boom generation, to lay aside self-interest for the sake of future generations, a commitment to honest thinking needs to underpin generous intentions. This pairing of honest thinking with generous or compassionate intentions is equivalent to being as wise as a serpent and as gentle as a dove. Honest thinking requires practice and astuteness, because it involves identifying and quizzing the way power is exercised; it also means being alert to the games we play to protect, promote and lie about ourselves and to ourselves.

Honest thinking:

- Does not blame.
- Acknowledges that the best we can hope for is to identify patterns and trends. Therefore our analysis will always involve an aspect of risk, and is necessarily humble.
- Acknowledges that our perceptions are partial and easily duped by the messages that we get from society.
- Recognizes that analysis has to be partnered with action if it is to be attested.

- Acknowledges personal responsibility because 'everything is connected to everything else'.
- Knows how the perception of vicious circles can easily dominate our view of the world, and therefore actively seeks out examples of virtuous processes. No predicament is so powerful that it is beyond resolution; otherwise honest thinking would be reduced to a counsel of despair.

This preamble on honest thinking is needed because, when mapping the journey from healthy self-esteem to mean-minded, ultra-selfish narcissism, we have to interrogate our own inner predilections, conflicts of interest and collapses of discipline. Only by tracking our own functioning do we gain insights into the choices available to us, as well as explore our motivation to change our behaviour. This conscious effort is essential because in an affluent society, saturated with advertising, we have to struggle to see and understand what is going on and to resist powerful messages which our *better self*[1] would wish to rebuff.

Once upon a time excessive narcissism was a hazard for the aristocratic or moneyed classes. Now, however, narcissism, or an over-developed self-regard, is likely to have infected most of us. This is the fear expressed by Christopher Lasch. In his view, a society which encourages individualism and self-gratification puts everyone at risk of narcissism, where self-regard topples over into selfishness and self-preoccupation. Twenge suggests that over the last twenty years narcissism has risen as much as obesity and the two may be related: both are due to our inability to control our desires.[2]

Narcissism is an unpleasant and disruptive state. Narcissists are said to be:

'overly focused on themselves and lack empathy for others, which means they cannot see another person's perspective and they also feel entitled to special privileges, and believe that they are superior people. As a result, narcissists are bad relationship partners and can be difficult to work with. Narcissists are also more likely to be hostile, feel anxious, compromise their health, and fight with friends and family.'[3]

The bad news is that the evidence suggests this toxic personality syndrome is growing. Twenge and her co-researchers investigated the growth of narcissism among American students. By comparing 1987 scores on the Narcissistic Personality Inventory with scores in 2006, they found that the *average* student score in 2006 was higher than 65 per cent of student scores in 1987. The data suggest that the number of college students scoring high on a measure of narcissism had increased to two-thirds in 2006. The evidence also points to narcissism being higher among young men, but between 2000 and 2006 the upward trend was rapid for young women.[4]

In relation to the generations, in the early 1950s only 12 per cent of teens agreed with the statement 'I am an important person', but by the late 1980s the figure had risen to 80 per cent. Commenting on these trends Twenge and Campbell note, 'Almost every trait related to narcissism rose between the 1950s and the 90s, including assertiveness, dominance, extraversion, self-esteem, and individualistic focus.'[5] The evidence suggests that the baby boomers were first to imbibe *en masse* narcissistic values, our offspring continued the unquestioned habit of 'self first', and as for the next generation, they have already been labelled 'Generation Me'.

The subtle power of films

In 2002, in the film 'Bend it like Beckham', Jess, an Asian-Indian girl living in London wants to play football. Her parents, already taken aback that their older daughter did not have an arranged marriage, want Jess, their younger daughter, to learn to cook and be a proper young lady. The plot comes to a head when Jess must shuttle back and forth between a football match and her sister's wedding. By the end of the movie Jess wants to join a professional women's football team and move to America to do so. Her parents, finally convinced that it's alright for Jess to follow her dreams, reluctantly agree.

The film is heart warming, and few can fail to be on the side of Jess, with her spontaneity and passion in comparison with the brittle, fusspot mentality of her parents, desperate to keep up appearances. It is easy to assume that virtue triumphs as Jess gets her wish. However the film, although on the surface about generational conflict between first and second generation immigrants, also dramatizes two interlocking changes: the fall of social rules and the rise of the individual, and as individualistic viewpoints become prominent, concern about the opinions of others plummets.[6] As we leave behind any concern about the opinion of others, then one of the most effective sanctions or constraints on our behaviour also falls away.

The TV series *Outnumbered* is hugely popular. The inventive thinking, insistence and sheer energy of the three children result in exhaustion and exasperation for their hard-pressed parents. The aspect of *Outnumbered* that mesmerizes the viewer is just how lifelike the children's performances are: surely no child actor can act so well? And there is the rub: the children are invited by the programme director to 'act naturally', and what we get are performances and vignettes that twist and turn around narcissistic characteristics. The demands the children make on their parents render *Outnumbered* a most effective contraceptive – who would want to have children? The risk is that the laughter and 'centre stageness' that is given to the youngsters will be contagious, and a generation of children will pick up the message that it is a fun and legitimate sport to outmanoeuvre your parents and demonstrate your superiority to them.

The parents in *Outnumbered* are far from young. True to life, they may have married when she was approaching thirty and he was approaching thirty-two, in accord with the statistics gathered by the Office for National Statistics on the average age of marriage in England and Wales in 2008. So harassed Mum and Dad are in the mid-forties, just that time of life when research suggests people are most likely to be maximally unhappy. It is the young and the old who are most likely to say they feel happy, consistently scoring higher on measures of wellbeing than those in their middle years. 'It is when you have all the burdens of middle age that your happiness level plummets. These are the people who bear the burdens of the intergenerational contract, with obligations to children and older people.'[7] And it has regularly made for scriptwriters' glee as tales of angst and misery make for mayhem, murder and marriage breakdown.

Thank God for the Single Life

Today roughly a third of the population lives alone. In part this is a product of older people who live alone due to the death of a partner, as well as the number, usually men, who live alone because of divorce. However, for as long as population statistics have been collected, never before have there been so many people living a single life, having never been married, and never having children. Having children is hard work. For previous generations having children was the natural consequence of sex and intimacy, however, over just two generations, the desire *and* capacity to limit the number of children to just one, or none, have been combined to great effect.

Not sure how I'll manage with two

As I sat in a café I overheard a conversation between three young women from a nearby office. One of them was pregnant and the conversation turned to whether she would return to work after her maternity leave. She reflected how she had been able to manage with her first child, but wondered whether she could cope with work and a second child, 'because I'll not just have two to get ready before I set off for work, I'll have to manage on only a few hours sleep each night as I have to feed the baby.' Later I heard the pregnant friend exclaim, 'You have so much fun, you two!'

As a working woman with no dependants I sometimes experience a pang of guilt when I think of the efforts and commitments of my fecund sisters. It occurs most often when I do the weekly shop in the evening in the local supermarket. One of the women on the checkouts is an acquaintance. I studiously avoid taking my purchases to her checkout. Why? Because she has three school-aged children. She works in the evening to fit in with family commitments and to earn what used to be called 'pin money' to help with the family budget. I also surmise that when she shops she selects all the 'basic' brands to cope with both the expense and the mega-appetite of three growing boys. In contrast, I review my shopping trolley and it contains 'top of the range' products. I reflect on this contrast and note that I am doubly blessed: comfortably off as many childless adults are, and grateful to the financially and emotionally hard-pressed parents who face up to the demands of child-rearing, and by so doing contribute to the means by which my future pension and care needs will be met. This is how I have organized my life and how I shall be borrowing from the future.

Having children changes people. The task of modern parenthood requires parents, especially mothers, to put their child's needs ahead of their own. Jonathan Franzen in his acclaimed novel on family life, *The Corrections*, makes the aside, 'We're all conditioned to think of our children as more important than us',[8] and this is right; society and maybe biology combine to make it such. This means that parenthood potentially challenges the inclination to please ourselves and give way to our own desires. As if on cue, Franzen also comments, 'What you discovered about yourself in raising children wasn't always agreeable or attractive.'[9] Franzen exposes and explores the personal battle of whether to put one's own needs and interests on hold, and allow the needs and interests of the child to take precedence, or whether to eschew parenthood altogether to continue the pursuit of other activities that bring satisfaction. This is where personal struggles get intertwined with wider societal dynamics. If younger generations are subject to media- and market-generated encouragements to be self-centred, and to see the world as revolving around them, *and* potential and actual parents have likewise received such encouragement, then family life is heading for collisions and calamity.

Bringing up a child now tops £200,000

The cost of bringing up a child has risen to more than £200,000 for the first time, according to a survey released in February 2010. Figures show the average parent is likely to have forked out more than £201,000 per child by the time their offspring has reached the age of 21. The cost has increased four per cent over the past year and 43 per cent in the seven years since the survey was first launched. The cost per year of bringing up a child is now highest during the university years following the introduction of tuition fees. It works out at £13,677 a year.

Campaigners said they were 'not surprised' at the results of the survey. Margaret Morrissey, from the pressure group Parents Outloud, said: 'Historically, you didn't have to expect to keep on raising a child until they were 21. You saw them through their schooling and that was it. The cost of them continuing with their education is extremely expensive.' She added that the cost did not always end at 21, either, as 'more and more youngsters were now returning to live with their parents after university as a result of the debts they had run up.'

Aggressive advertising aimed at children also made its mark on parents' pockets. 'Ten-year-old children are totally aware of all the things that you have to have to keep up with the other children and it's very difficult for parents to stand out against them,' Ms Morrissey added. 'Even if a school encourages its pupils to cycle to school in the interests of the environment, it costs in terms of the latest designer bicycle or scooter.'

The survey covered nearly 4,000 adults and was carried out during January 2010. Perhaps unsurprisingly, parents in outer London faced the biggest cost in raising a child – £220,769. Yorkshire and Humberside was the cheapest place at £177,706.[10]

The average number of births per woman is low in many European nations both because women are not having children and because of the move towards later marriage. The usual explanation for this is the difficulty of entering the housing market and coping with insecure employment, which combine to make for a slow and later commencement in starting a family. However, there is another factor: 'Modern women were raised to be Bridget Jones, not mothers. The arrival of a baby prompts a massive conflict between Bridget's mother identity, and her worker and consumer ones.'[11] The options now available to women are many, with motherhood only one of them, and not only is parenthood arduous and expensive, motherhood it is a bumpy emotional journey.

The risk is that women get blamed for not having children and therefore causing all kinds of disruption to society. This finger pointing would be wrong, as finger pointing always is. The issue is more complex and it is both a personal and a political issue. As social rules lose their leverage and people, not just women, are no longer rule-bound, then the fragmentation that results threatens the social obligations that tie society together. Instead of honouring social obligations we drift towards a society in which it is everyone for themselves from birth to death. However, as well as making for a miserable life 'here and now', such an individualized ethic easily shrugs off any responsibility for future generations.

Learning from the gay community: Self-restrained individualism

One of the most explicit shaking free of the constraints of social rules is that achieved by the gay movement. Within a generation being gay has become an accepted lifestyle. The

Pink Pound is only occasionally called upon to meet the cost of raising a family, and the combined remuneration of two adults without dependents can seem to offer a most desirable lifestyle, especially in comparison to the chaotic and manic spectacle depicted in the *Outnumbered* household. The loss of constraining social rules that has given permission for people to live as gay is a further factor in low fertility levels, especially in western nations. The image of a gay lifestyle that is often promoted is one of indulgence, decadence *and narcissism*. What is less noted is the frequent commitment of those who are gay to the voluntary or third sector, and that includes a commitment to the Church.

The issues of individuality and choice, and the casual and sometimes deliberate letting go of social rules or norms, are all closely related. Those who are 'out and proud' gay have made a conscious and on occasion a costly decision to step outside social norms. But instead of this triggering a mode of individuality that speaks of 'everyone for themselves from birth to death', for many who have 'come out' their wider life choices speak of a concern for the wellbeing of others. How else to explain the tendency of gays and lesbians to have long careers in public service, especially in the more arduous and less well-rewarded voluntary and community sector? This commitment to the public good is key because it is undertaken by those who, in other areas of their lives, have thrown off social convention in the pursuit of self-interest. Those who have made a choice to pursue same-sex partnerships may lead the way in showing how shaking off social rules does not have to mean denial of social responsibility.

This is an example of *self-restrained individualism*. By this I mean that each of us, despite shrugging off social rules in relation to some aspects of our lives, can limit or restrain our pursuit of self-interest and self-indulgence in other areas of our lives. A case can be made that such self-restrained individualism represents an exceptional level of moral behaviour, because self-limitation is chosen rather than forced upon us by social rules and norms. An important role of faith is to help people to establish for themselves how to contain their personal freedom. This contrasts with earlier Christian practice, where the Church dictated and enforced self-restraint in order to counter any inclination towards independence of thought and individualism.

In Chapter Four I suggest a five-point constellation that constitutes *second chance theology*[12] and that connects with the extensive individualism and rule-averse characteristics that have developed in our society. The five points at the heart of second chance theology permit and even encourage individualism and an enhanced recognition of one's uniqueness, but they also provide a counterbalance that enables us to limit our freedom and self-centredness. These five points that enable self-restrained individualism can be summarized:

- a sense of self that speaks of uniqueness and preciousness in the sight of God
- an imperative towards compassion
- acknowledgement of the implications of the conscious and unconscious dastardliness that taints all that we do
- acknowledgement of the importance of forgiveness both for ourselves and for forgiving others
- confidence that deep and enabling benevolence permeates the whole of creation; this is to acknowledge the terrain of classical theology that speaks of grace and the Holy Spirit

These five points are amplified by the teaching and the way in which Jesus lived his life. They are offered as a 'constellation' which is but a small subset of all the theological insights that are available to us. These five points that make up second chance theology are deliberately *sin-lite*, because sin is a tricky concept in a culture that invests in individualism and legitimizes the pursuit of pleasure and self-fulfilment. However, this 'sin-lite' approach is moderated by an emphasis on *struggle*, in that it becomes essential to struggle for insight and self-discipline amidst the vast array of conflicting voices and ideas, and this struggle is more than a struggle of the intellect or the emotion: it is a struggle at the level of the soul.

It is bold to suggest that an emphasis on struggle can supersede an emphasis on sin. Sin is so much associated with Church and being a Christian that it can be shocking to have sin relegated to a lower league, not least because for some the *raison d'etre* of Jesus was to conquer the power of sin by dying on the cross and rising to new life. And for centuries, if not millennia, social rules have been kept in place by describing their breaching as sin, and sin leads to hellfire and damnation. We know this riff, but it no longer works; in fact, no longer do any threats of a religious nature work. The new riff, while not denying the salvation that comes from Jesus' death and resurrection, puts the emphasis on Jesus saving us by showing us how to live, and in examining how Jesus lived, or 'performed', we see the extent to which 'struggle' was a part of his life.

William Bouwsma also proposes that commitment to struggle is an essential element of the Christian faith and that the avoidance of or quitting from struggle is the very worst state into which humankind can fall. In this Bouwsma also shifts the emphasis away from sin, and he does this straightforwardly. He notes that a central tenet of the Christian faith is that sins can be forgiven. To resist 'struggle', however, is to deny the call to creativity and compassion made by

God. Furthermore, Bouwsma suggests that commitment to struggle, the struggle that is deeper than intellect and emotion, and is a struggle at the level of the soul, is an essential feature of maturity, both for those who embrace a Christian faith and those who do not.[13] This emphasis on struggle resonates with insights from evolutionary biologists, who recognize that if a species is to thrive, members of the species must enter fully into a struggle against the raw abrasive aspects of life. It is this insight from evolutionary biology that thrusts us back into the vexed issue of narcissism.

Homo sapiens needs religion for psychological health: A summary of the thinking of Ernest Becker in his groundbreaking book *The Denial of Death*

Ernest Becker, in his book *The Denial of Death*, suggests that we have been set adrift by our analytical strengths. In particular our modern minds have been able to banish mystery as unreal, and dismiss religious belief as naiveté. Our thinking veers towards 'cause and effect' and the logical always trumps the mysterious. (Here we have echoes of the distinction between formal and dialectical operations discussed in Chapter Five).

This fixation on what is measurable and material means that we are unable to make the lonely leap into faith, i.e. achieving personal trust in some kind of transcendent support for one's life. In a culture which only values the logical and causality, and religious teaching no longer convinces, we get marooned in our deep sense of being special. In the absence of anything worthy enough to give hope, or robust or big enough to be trustworthy, Becker suggests we become, 'A miserable animal, whose body decays, who will die, who will pass into dust and

---

oblivion, disappear for ever not only in this world but in all the possible dimensions of the universe, whose life serves no conceivable purpose.'[14]

Embracing a religious faith requires us to expand ourselves trustingly into the non-logical, into the terrain that is truly beyond belief. This spiritual expansion is something that advanced modern people find difficult, especially as there are no longer any collective dramas or narratives that can be shared. The absence of such props means there is little to help the non-religious to have a *deep* confidence in their sense of being special, and thus a neurotic insistence on being unique in the universe, and solely worthy, gains an unhealthy momentum.

Becker suggests that the species Homo sapiens has always been neurotic, but there are some environments where it is possible to manage one's neurotic impulses adequately. The problem now, Becker suggests, is there is no embracing worldview that a secularized person can depend on to provide 'some kind of affirmative collective ideology in which the person can perform the living drama of his acceptance as a creature.'[15] In historic terms the post–1960s era has provided little to enable the neurotic narcissist to come out of his or her isolation and embrace a larger and higher wholeness in the way that religion offers.

Becker, like other depth psychologists, suggests that the defeat of despair is not principally an intellectual problem. Desolation and despondency are not helped by 'more knowing'; rather, it is only by more living and doing, in a manner that enables self-forgetfulness that these life-denying states can be conquered. Becker quotes Goethe: 'We must plunge into experience and then reflect on the meaning of it. All reflection and no plunging drives us mad; all plunging and no reflection and we are brutes.'[16]

Becker draws on the work of Otto Rank[17] to locate a 'cure' for neurosis in 'legitimate foolishness' that transforms natural and excessive neurosis into creative living. The 'cure' that both Rank and Becker identify is religion, and Christianity in particular can answer the hero mentality that besets us all. Religion today (unlike earlier periods in human history) is a freely-chosen dependency that provides shelter from narcissistic neurosis by:

- enabling pre-occupation with personal power to be superseded by God in the cosmos
- freedom from the need to keep pleasing (following) those around us, because of the scope to 'please' God, thus allowing for independent values that are enfolded within the context of a God who loves justice, mercy and holiness
- embracing ideals that lead us on and beyond ourselves.

Finally Becker suggests that religion solves the problem of death by enabling the 'hero' to surrender themselves to the reality of nature taking its toll, and by enabling the sense of an expanded self, closer to God, to continue. In allowing the person to face up to the reality of death, then a door is opened into the possibility of hope. Becker writes: 'Religion alone keeps hope, because it holds open the dimension of the unknown and the unknowable, the fantastic mystery of creation that the human mind cannot even begin to approach, the possibility of a multidimensionality of existence, of heavens and possible embodiments that make a mockery of earthly logic – and in doing so, it relieves the absurdity of earthly life, all the impossible limitations and frustrations of living matter.'[18]

Ernest Becker died from cancer at the age of 49, two months before his Pulitzer Prize winning book The Denial of Death *was published.*

Three steps to ruination?

Narcissism is not just a lifestyle trait. It is a route to ruination, not just because it makes us psychologically unhealthy and spoils relationships; it is more dangerous still and those who study evolution know this. Alister Hardy studied marine biology as a means of understanding evolutionary forces. Hardy died in 1985; he had lived through a tumultuous century, a century marked by world wars but which was also characterized by growth in affluence and the growth of technology. Drawing on the insights gathered from his experience, he feared that the species Homo sapiens was at risk of entering an evolutionary cul-de-sac, and would follow the route of many species, which after a brief period of flourishing would collapse into extinction. His reason for this dire assessment was the ease with which the species used its energy and creativity to *avoid* the struggle of grappling with the raw and abrasive aspects of life. Aldous Huxley, likewise, hypothesized that what we love will ruin us because we have been captivated by the pursuit of comfort and pleasure-seeking. Narcissism, or excessive self-love, especially when combined with the dynamics of a global market, gives birth to extensive decadence which avoids at all costs rubbing up against the raw and abrasive aspects of life.

This is the sternest of warnings to those who care for the future. Already it is possible to see the most poignant of ruinations: the formation of people unable to sustain love because of being so caught up in self-love that they are unable to love another. 'Love is primarily giving, not receiving.'[19] This means that to love involves a readiness to abandon self-concern and self-indulgence. Loving involves giving away one's self for the sake of another. It cannot be done instrumentally; it has to be entered into with an openness that allows the 'other' to be more central than the self. This is a tough call for those eaten away by narcissism. As narcissism becomes extensive, younger generations are caught in a fearsome trap, where love is the thing most desired and yet also most feared. Commitment becomes virtually impossible because of the unquenchable demands of an insistent 'me'. This is a dastardly state of affairs, because to be fully human is to be able to express love and commitment to another.

The second ruination tripwire is falling for the deceit that the pursuit of plenty provides a route to wellbeing. Evidence is growing that 'plenty' doesn't make for happiness. Having everything we want, especially when combined with narcissism, makes us miserable. Intuitively we have always sensed this to be the case, however, the work of Martin Seligman and other positive psychologists now provides copious amounts of evidence to support this intuition. For younger people the mismatch between lofty expectations of getting and having and the disappointing reality can be harsh. In the absence of any other motivation for life, this existential predicament is reflected in the growing rates of suicide among young people.[20]

The changing pattern of suicide

The World Health Organization estimates that over the last 45 years suicide rates have increased by 60 per cent worldwide, and is the third most frequent cause of death for those aged 15–44 (male and female). Although suicide rates have traditionally been highest among elderly men, rates among young people have been increasing to such an extent that they are now the group at highest risk in a third of all countries. [21]

The third tripwire that leads to ruination was expounded by Ernest Becker in his Pulitzer Prize-winning book *The Denial of Death*. The main thesis of his book is that 'The idea of death, the fear of it, haunts the human animal like nothing else.'[22] Becker suggests that this deep-seated fear, unless addressed, contributes to a sickness at the very heart of the individual and society. He writes:

'We have learned, mostly from Alfred Adler, that what man needs most is to feel secure in his self-esteem. But man is not just a blind glob of idling protoplasm, but a creature with a name who lives in the world of symbols and dreams and not merely matter. His sense of self-worth is constituted symbolically, his cherished narcissism feeds on symbols, on an abstract idea of his own worth... In childhood, we see the struggle for self-esteem at its least disguised. The child is unashamed about what he needs and wants most. His whole organism shouts the claims of his natural narcissism. And this claim can make childhood hellish for the adults concerned, especially when there are several children competing at once for the prerogatives of limitless self-extension, what we might call 'cosmic significance'. The term is not meant to be taken lightly... at the heart of the creature is the desire to stand out, to be *the* one in creation. When you combine natural narcissism with the basic need for self-esteem, you create a creature who has to feel himself an object of primary value: first in the universe, representing in himself all of life.'[23]

However, this person of 'primary value' who sees and experiences him or herself as first in the universe, will one day die and disappear for ever, and this is a terrifying predicament.

Living psychologically beyond our means

It would seem that we are not just living beyond our economic capacity; we are also living beyond our psychological capacity in our inclination to 'limitless self expansion'.[24] It is in relation to this that religion matters. We are familiar with the role of religion in providing reassurance about death not being the end of life, and this has led to religions being criticized as little more that immortality formulas. What is less acknowledged is that religions address this inclination to live beyond our psychological means. It is easy to despise narcissistic people, only to discover that the inclination to despise often has its roots in the same psychological failing. We are all saps, vulnerable to the mood music that surrounds us, easily addicted and besotted by celebrity and selfishness. Such fragility is not limited to an age group, or to a particular gender or sexuality.

Religion has traditionally reduced the likelihood of narcissism; Jewish and Christian scripture is full of the pitfalls that can befall the proud and full of commendations for those who are humble and forgiving. Narcissists are certainly not humble and are likely to be slow to forgive. It is to this plight that the Christian faith speaks. Historically, it has been the empowerment that comes from faith that has helped people to muster the determination to change both their attitudes and their behaviour. There have been times when the process of 'church' has achieved this. Early Methodism and the early days of the Salvation Army were extraordinary facilitators of people changing their attitudes and behaviour, and being sustained by their involvement in these expressions of church. In countering narcissism and its carelessness towards the future, we can draw confidence from this exceptional achievement, as well as from recognition that the species Homo sapiens, although psychologically flawed, is also characterized by zest, adaptability and stamina.

There are echoes here of Bahro's assertion that when a culture becomes sickly, a new culture is created by a few people who are not afraid to be insecure.'[25] Those few people will be those who have a sense that their life has meaning, and know the feasibility of engaging in intentional behaviour in the pursuit of this meaning in their lives. Early Methodism and Salvationism pioneered just this. They fostered within people the ability to make sense of their actions within a larger frame: 'God'. This in turn brought vital motivation to embrace the intentional activity that enabled people to resist becoming *victims* of troublesome circumstances. This is not some fantasy; historically this example from early Methodism shows how religious commitment enabled the new industrial proletariat to face the challenges of the burgeoning industrial order, and prepared the ground for a later socialism.

Some commentators suggest that the impact of Methodism created revolution in Britain. Revolution is a rare historical state. It involves throwing off the perceived constraints of circumstance and taking up new intentional activity both individually and corporately. Revolution involves the transformation of values and approaches, bringing new ways of seeing and a new way of organizing. Revolution also involves a shift in the balance of power away from the status quo. Methodism accomplished this amongst 'the anxious, the dislocated, the rootless, the disturbed',[26] achieving what Alberto Melucci considers to be the longed-for aim of the current panoply of social movements: the achievement of a passionate commitment to change our culture, and the structures of our culture, and to redefine ourselves in the present by recognizing that past choices and decisions are reversible.[27]

We are not prisoners of our past, we have the capacity to resist the norms and sanctions on our behaviour, and we are a species with a capacity for compassionate intentionality. What we need is a new framework within which these capacities can find their expression. The capacity of baby boomers to be the dissenters from the march towards ever greater narcissism is critical, not just for future generations; but it may be vital for the future of the species itself.

Taking hold of the life that really is life

There is great gain in godliness combined with contentment; for we brought nothing into the world, so we can take nothing out of it... Those who want to be rich fall into temptation and are trapped by many senseless and harmful desires that plunge people into ruin and destruction. For the love of money is the root of all kinds of evil, and in their eagerness to be rich some wandered away from the faith and pierced themselves with many pains. But as for you, man of God, shun all this; pursue righteousness, godliness, faith, love, endurance, gentleness... It is God alone who has immortality and dwells in an unapproachable light, whom no one has ever seen or can see... As for those who in the present age are rich, command them not to be haughty, or to set their hopes on the uncertainty of riches, but rather on God who richly provides us with everything for our enjoyment. They are to do good, to be rich in good works, generous and ready to share, thus storing up for themselves the treasure of a good foundation for the future, so that they may take hold of the life that really is life.

St Paul in his first Letter to Timothy[28]

Notes

1. The issue of whether, as Homo sapiens, we have an urge to develop a more moral self is critical and rarely considered, other than via the battle lines drawn up around Richard Dawkins' case for *The Selfish Gene*. Allahyari takes another approach to the issue by researching the motivation of those who volunteer to work on behalf of homeless people (See R. A. Allahyari (2000) *Visions of Charity*, California: University of California Press). The implications of Allahyari's concept of 'moral-selving' is explored in my book *Journeying Out* (1997) London: Continuum; see Chapter 10.

2. J. M. Twenge and W. K. Campbell (2009) *The Narcissism Epidemic*, New York: Free Press p.31.

3. J. M. Twenge (2006) *Generation Me*, New York: Free Press p.68–9.

4. Ibid. p.69.

5. J. M. Twenge and W. K. Campbell (2009) op.cit. p.33.

6. Adapted from J. M. Twenge (2006) op. cit. p.21.

7. D. Willetts (2010) *The Pinch*, London: Atlantic Books p. 119.

8. J. Franzen (2001) *The Corrections*, New York: Farrar, Straus and Giroux, p.302.

9. Ibid. p.261.

10. From R. Garner 'Bringing up a child now tops £200,000, if you're lucky...' the *Independent, Tuesday, 23 February 2010.*

11. O. James 'Are you an Organizer, a Hugger or a Fleximum?' in the *Guardian* (Family Supplement) *3rd April 2010* p. 2.

12. Second chance theology aims to re-introduce theology to those who may have previously written off or dismissed Christian teaching and insights.

13. W. Bouwsma, 'Christian Adulthood' in E. Erikson (ed.) *Adulthood*, New York: Norton, 1978.

14. E. Becker (1973) *The Denial of Death*, New York: The Free Press p. 201.

15. Ibid p. 198.

16. Ibid p. 199.

17. Otto Rank, a psychotherapist working at the beginning of the twentieth century, never founded a school of psychotherapy as such, but influenced the work of Fromm, Horney and Adler as well as Becker. In particular Becker draws on Rank's consideration of the artist and artistic creativity. 'On the one hand', Rank says, 'the artist has a particularly strong tendency towards glorification of his own will. Unlike the rest of us, he feels compelled to remake reality in his own image. And

yet a true artist also needs immortality, which he can only achieve by identifying himself with the collective will of his culture and religion. Good art could be understood as a joining of the material and the spiritual, the specific and the universal, or the individual and humanity.' From www.http://webspace.ship.edu/cgboer/rank.html.

18. E. Becker (1973) op.cit. p. 203–4.

19. E. Fromm (1995) *The Art of Loving*, New York: Thorsons p.18.

20. Suicide rates for young men had been falling in the UK. This must be credited to the efforts of mental health services in response to a government target to reduce suicide in general and among young men in particular. However, the impact of tough economic times has been to send the statistics on an upward curve.

21. See World Health Organization www.who.int/mental_health/prevention/suicide/country_reports/en/+%22World+Health+Organisation%22+suicide+rates.

22. E. Becker (1973) op.cit. p. ix.

23. E. Becker (1973) op.cit. pp. 2–3.

24. This point is made by Sigmund Freud in 'Thoughts for the Times on War and Death', (1915), *Collected Papers*, vol. 4, New York: Basic Books, (1959) pp. 316–7.

25. This quotation is not referenced on the website of the Northumbria Community http://www.northumbriacommunity.org/.

26. B. Semmel (1973) *The Methodist Revolution*, London: Heinemann p.7.

27. A. Melucci (1989). *Nomads of the Present: Social Movements and Individual Needs in Contemporary Society*, Philadelphia: Temple University Press.

28. Adapted from 1 Timothy vv. 6–16 NRSV.

CHAPTER NINE

Pivot: Paying our proper dues

If we baby boomers are to be a pivot generation that reduces our need to borrow from future generations, this will involve more than a transfer of money and wealth. As an older generation there are additional dues that need to be paid. These proper, appropriate dues fall into three categories:

- commitment to political action to lobby for policies that favour younger generations
- alertness to the ease with which we can drift into selfishness and self-preoccupation in later life and be a wearisome pain to others, especially younger generations
- exercising due diligence about the pursuit of the human strengths and virtues that have a beneficial outcome in relation to later life.

Taking the political issue first, Ed Howker and Shiv Malik, in their book *The Jilted Generation: How Britain has bankrupted its youth*, describe the antics of politicians in relation to generational fairness as a 'conspiracy of the cowardly'.[1] They observe the dual messages that politicians give to young and old: 'Young people must shape up; old people must be valued more highly'.[2] They also examine the idea that a generation can act consciously to shape the future of a nation. They conclude that this is unlikely, and therefore the current inequality between the generations does not result from a conspiracy by baby boomers secretly to control British politics. Their argument takes a different direction.

Howker and Malik suggest that the debate about fairness between the generations obscures the really big issue: 'The dawning of a new age of self-expression and the spread of a philosophy of individualism that (has) completely reshaped Britain's politics.'[3] Their analysis, with its echo of the increasing prevalence of narcissism, is that the vast majority of us are *consumers who want to be individuals* and that politicians in turn, relate to the electorate as individual consumers motivated by self-interest, which makes the political task that of responding to what people want. The justification for this is that people know best what they want. As a consequence long-term interests are ignored, including neglect of the wellbeing of our children's children.

The advice of a pollster

'I felt that the most important thing for (Bill Clinton) to do was to bring to the political system the same consumer rules/ philosophy as the business community has. Because what politics needs to be is responsive to the whims and the desires of the marketplace as business is, and it needs to be as sensitive to the bottom line – profit or votes – as a business is.'[4]

The suggestion to my own generation that we become a 'pivot' generation is not just for the sake of our children's children. It represents the restoration of one of the proper responsibilities of politics, that of putting the future at its heart.

This is not the place to explore the insights of political and economic philosophers such as Hume or Smith, or to explore the Aristotelian principles of 'just desert'. For Christians there is a simple but uncomfortable truth that makes it essential to ensure that the future is taken into account, and it is that Jesus died for all mankind and this makes all people, past, present and future, equal in the sight of God.

It is a challenge to the imagination, as much as to our moral stretch, to give the future a high priority. Every one of us will be familiar with the way in which the pressing invariably crowds out the important. For the future to have the same standing in our priorities as the immediate, not only does self-interest have to be eschewed, so too the imagination needs to be harnessed to devise new approaches and strategies. Nowhere is this more critical than in relation to the impact the ageing of our population is having on democratic processes. If demography is not to trump democracy, then my generation of baby boomers has to forego self-interest and vote for the future wellbeing of our children's children. This will mean devising new methods of raising revenue from older people *and* lobbying for such developments.

This need for different forms of taxation may be in step with environmental concerns. For example, Phillippe Legrande suggests we should 'Tax harmful things, such as carbon emissions.' So baby boomers will need to face up to saying 'Amen' to that. He also suggests introducing a Land Value tax, and baby boomers will need to face up to saying 'Amen' to this as well. Legrande notes that income tax, because it is a tax on work, is wasteful, as the incentive is to work less, and no tax is raised on the lost output. In contrast, land is in fixed supply and impossible to avoid. In Britain we seem addicted to property speculation and are not put off by the regular occurrence of a property 'bubble', but:

'swapping more or less the same stock of houses with each other cannot logically create riches for society as a whole. Indeed, it has huge costs because it diverts funds from productive investment – while the resulting boom and bust, as we know, can cause havoc. Taxing land could curb property bubbles, and encourage productive investment elsewhere… and no matter how heavily you tax it land cannot be spirited away to a tax haven.'[5]

Legrande points to places such as Hong Kong, Singapore and Denmark where there is land value taxation, and low income tax as a result. With so many advantages it is surprising that it is not on the government's agenda, especially as it is a progressive tax because the distribution of land is very unequal.[6] Perhaps the reason is that politicians of whatever party would anticipate an unholy coalition of the landed and the middle classes raising their voices in opposition. If the baby boomer generation could get serious about being a pivot generation, then there would be an alternative cry, a cry for fairness over self-interest, that politicians would have to take into account in their policy making.

Inheritance tax takes us in to fraught terrain. It is one of the most divisive factors in our society. Richard Reeves, the former Director of Demos and now political adviser to Nick Clegg, does not pull his punches when he writes about the ethical issue at the heart of inheritance tax:

'The boomers' children might want their windfall, but this is morally undeserving, as it is unrelated to their effort or talent. Protecting the rights of the affluent to slosh their money down the next generation should not be a priority for any government.'[7]

We baby boomers have done well out of the property market and we have also benefited from a favourable tax regime when a mortgage was tax allowable. If we baby boomers are to be genuine about our intention to provide a pivot on which the balance of advantage can be shifted towards the generations still to come, then we will have to learn to welcome hefty taxation on even a modest estate. In the new map of life that we are negotiating, those of us with property assets should make friends with the possibility that our property becomes collateral to meet the cost of a long old age, rather than a nest egg for the children. It will not be popular, but it is one of our new dues, given the extent to which our longevity will add to our need to borrow from the future.

We are used to national and local government taking money from us, but there is also scope to give back to government what it gives to us. The classic distinction, in relation to public benefits, is between those that are universal and those that are means-tested. There is scope for a third category: benefits that are universal but with scope for them to be returned, literally *sent back*, saying, 'thanks, but no thanks'. Even if only one in a thousand chose to act in this way, it would make for a great discussion point and raise awareness of this 'present versus the future' debate, especially if 'my entitlement returned with thanks' could be specifically deployed for some future benefit. Whilst this may be a naïve suggestion, nonetheless in helping to promote the message that 'the future is as important as the present' then it has a role, not least because it gives us all-important practice in recognising and acknowledging that we already have enough.

It would take a brave government to set up a 'return of entitlement' facility for fear of mockery. Such a provision would be like a 'moral gym' enabling us to limber up and test for ourselves the religious and psychological insights which emphasize that 'by giving we receive', and that wellbeing is rooted in meaningfulness and self-forgetfulness, rather than in more and more wealth. Returning our entitlements 'with thanks' could provide a third option to universal or means-tested benefits, and might just lessen the need for universal entitlements to become means-tested ones, and save those who really need the entitlement a lot of hassle.

Bye Buy Test

Use this test when shopping to think about what or who is influencing your choices:

Why do I want to buy it?
How often will I use it?
Can I afford it?
What will happen if I don't buy it?

From the Mothers' Union Campaign 'Bye Buy Childhood'

One has to be astute if one is to lobby for policies that favour younger generations, because such policies come under many guises. While policies in relation to education and child welfare are easy to spot, policies in relation to maternity leave will be described as a women's issue, and housing policy may be presented as a poverty issue, but both have a disproportionate impact on younger compared to older people. We are familiar with assessing policies in relation to their impact on the wealthy and those who are poor, or the squeezed middle, referring to the middle or lower middle or professional classes. We need to become equally adept at assessing the impact along generational lines, and more even than this, to work out whether it is affordable without borrowing from the future. Working out the extent to which public policy borrows from the future requires serious discernment. However, there is one guise in relation to this which is easy to expose, and that is the mantra that we have to spend our way out of the recession – making 'buying stuff' a moral obligation. This is short-termism dressed up as economic strategy. If we are to express concern for the future, we have to be tough minded and recognize that there will be personal costs, and furthermore, we shall face criticism for this off-centre approach.

Finally, we all have to weigh up (yes, that is code for our personal cost-benefit analysis) the merits of you or me, potentially aged 97, receiving the costly care of an intensive or coronary care ward, compared with the care needed for a youngster with leukaemia. Perhaps this is a false dichotomy, but I refer to it because the likelihood is that by the time we baby boomers reach our fourth age, then 'advanced direc-tives' regarding our future medical treatment and care will be mandatory. We will be required to be explicit about how we wish our final days on this earth to be resolved. It is not wise to leave such considerations until the crisis is upon us. This 'weighing up' is not just a calculation for the health econo-mists, although we may wish to consult their calculations; it is for each of us to make, and at the heart of this calculation we will need to factor in our responsibility to future generations. This issue is so significant that I have made it the subject of the next chapter.

On not being a pain

A religious sister said to me recently that she felt she had a responsibility to keep herself as well and as active as she could

– for the sake of others. She considered she had a responsibility not to be a burden on others and, more even than this, to shelter younger sisters from the task of caring for those for whom she was exercising care. Many older people will identify with this, wanting more than anything to grow old without becoming a burden on their children. Usually this burdensomeness is thought of in terms of health, but there are other ways in which being old can make younger friends and relatives weary. The hazard of later life is that we become even more self-preoccupied in response to the circumstances in which many of us will grow old. Each of us has to decide how miserable and tetchy we are going to allow ourselves to become. There is a choice, because there is growing insight into what makes for emotional wretchedness and what we can do to protect ourselves from falling prey to such a wearisome state.

Loneliness is the most frequent trigger for wretchedness. Loneliness can be damaging at any stage in the lifespan, but it can be most unrelenting in later life. It is in later life that the companionship which has given sustenance for decades can be shattered by death or dementia. The combination of loss and loneliness can be a heavy and dreaded burden. Loneliness is a debilitating emotion, so much so that its impact shows up when measuring stress hormones, immune resistance and cardio-vascular function. Loneliness is even linked to more rapid progress of Alzheimer's disease.[8] All these things are in addition to loneliness having a negative impact on behaviour. Loneliness has such a disruptive impact that it works against its resolution. Even when offered the opportunity for social encounters, including with loved ones, when we are pained by loneliness, it can be hard to resist lashing out verbally at those who make an effort to come close. This is the nasty feature of loneliness; it can develop into a self-reinforcing loop of negative thoughts and behaviour, because when we are lonely we are more likely to make a mess of the opportunities to connect when they do come along.

Homo sapiens needs to be connected with others; we are a social species, although as we grow older our capacity for solitude, in fact our desire for solitude, increases. But even so, a lack of social connectedness can undermine our ability to think clearly, because we are less likely to be able to see things from the point of view of another, or to evaluate their intentions. Loneliness can 'force us into a defensive crouch (that) can also cost us some of our ability to self-regulate'.[9] In other words we might, more than anything, want to be welcoming and expansive in our encounter, but get caught up in sarcasm and tetchiness, wrecking the possibility of a good experience that both parties would wish to repeat. Verbal barbs and verbal assaults can be a feature of intergenerational communication, and they are wearying and best kept under close control for everyone's sake. This following conversation, which occurred 'in passing', illustrates the ease with which this can happen, and it especially happens across the generations:

Acquaintance: 'How nice to see you. Oh, and these must be your grandchildren – oh, and your daughter, How lovely.'

Grandmother: 'Oh yes, they are staying for the weekend – not long enough! (Biff!) They came on Friday evening, that's why I couldn't get to the hotpot supper (Bash!).'

This exchange I describe as a *biff-bash* conversation. An ageing mother had her visiting daughter in her sights, except that more than anything she would have wished she could have held back from biffing and bashing. It was a conversation to which three generations were party, although those in the middle and youngest generation were listeners only. It is not just contributors to conversations who can find themselves wincing at the direction a conversation takes, but those who happen to be nearby. This 20-second conversation illustrates how loneliness can develop into a self-reinforcing loop.

My guess is that the grandmother in this conversation was caught between the delight of having her extended family alongside, but at a deeper level she was angry that such delight, and reassurance and support, was exceptional rather than routine. We all do it, not just grandmothers. We find ways of niggling others by the things we say, half aware and relishing the impact of our words, and half wishing that we had never said them. Perhaps it is down to insensitivity, but very often it is linked with loneliness. Corrosive conversations such as these are an indication of how difficult it is to self-regulate when we are afflicted by loneliness.

Philip Larkin tutors his lover in relation to conversation...

'Dear, I must seem very pompous and huffy, with my portentous hints and veiled criticisms of you, and I wonder you are so patient. But for all that, I do want to urge you, with all love and kindness, to think about how much you say and how you say it. I'd even go so far as to make three rules: One, never say more than two sentences, or very rarely three, without waiting for an answer or comment from whoever you're talking to; Two, abandon altogether your harsh didactic voice, and use only the soft musical one (except in special cases); and Three, don't do more than glance at your interlocutor (wrong word?) once or twice while speaking. You're getting a habit of boring your face up or round into the features of your listener – don't do it! It's most trying. You notice I don't say anything about what you say – I don't mind that – these simple points of technique are what I want to urge on you, because I've thought about it for ages, and finally I decided that my feelings are abstractly just and not a personal foible. I think you'd get on much better all round if you took yourself in hand in this direction.… Anyway, to things pleasanter…'[10]

Being able to handle the assault of loneliness is an important aspect of being a 'pivot' generation, because it is not just a case of lessening the financial burden on future generations; the emotional pressures we load on younger generations also have to be lessened. Given our probable longevity, we shall accompany our children for a very long time, and as we are likely to have had only one or two children, the yoke they face will be heavy. An extreme illustration of this comes from China, where, as a result of the one child policy, a young adult, often a young man, is likely to be overshadowed by six relatives – two parents and four grandparents – for a very long period of his life. With such a spectre, we who are likely to be old for a very long time have a responsibility to spare the younger generations the bruising from the emotional cosh wielded with such precision by elders, unable to self-regulate because of chronic loneliness.

Conversation is vital as an aide to negotiating the extraordinary new map of life that confronts us. We need conversations that enable us to mull over the perceptions and experiences we have of ageing to 'gain reassurance of their validity and significance.'[11] We need reassurance because our perception and experience of ageing will be at odds with the perceptions of ageing that have prevailed throughout history. We need to talk about ageing if we are to answer the fundamental question of the third age:

'How are we going to use this sudden, unprecedented, unanticipated release from mortality? How are we to conduct ourselves now that all of us can expect to live out something like the full natural span?'[12]

It is through conversation that we are able to express our ideas and feelings. More than ever, as pioneer explorers of the new map of life, older people need opportunities to hear themselves think and explore how their experiences may resonate with others. Mary Wolfe comments that:

'Through conversation we turn around our ideas and experiences with each other ... and we thereby also review those ideas and experiences ... conversation provides us with one way in which either to revisit our experiences or to entertain possibilities of future experiences.'[13]

If opportunities for conversation are few then we talk to ourselves; we ruminate, turning an event or a notion over and over in our mind, and in the process perspective and proportion easily get lost. Rumination is similar to worry, except rumination focuses on bad feelings and experiences from the past, whereas worry tends to focus on potential bad events in the future. Ruminating is unhealthy, it adds to anxiety and it can make for depression as we continually review a troubling event. Talking helps, except that so often, as a result of re-playing an event over and over in our mind, the opportunity to talk is squandered because the pressure has built up to such a level that 'it comes out wrong'. Loneliness increases the likelihood of ruminating, especially for women.[14] However, it is easier to address ruminating than it is to address loneliness, so this makes for a good place to start reducing the risk of piling our emotional baggage onto younger generations.

There are skills to learn that can counter ruminating and these skills need time to master. They also highlight the importance of valuing solitude, a close cousin of loneliness; however there is a world of difference between the two. Hara Estroff Marano describes the difference:

'From the outside, solitude and loneliness look a lot alike. Both are characterized by solitariness. But all resemblance ends at the surface. Loneliness is a negative state, marked by a sense of isolation. One feels that something is missing. It is possible to be with people and still feel lonely – perhaps the most bitter form of loneliness. Solitude is the state of being alone without being lonely ... Solitude is a time that can be used for reflection, inner searching or growth or enjoyment of some kind. Deep reading requires solitude, so does experiencing the beauty of nature. Thinking and creativity usually do too.

Solitude suggests peacefulness stemming from a state of inner richness. It is a means of enjoying the quiet and whatever it brings that is satisfying and from which we draw sustenance. It is something we cultivate. Solitude is refreshing, an opportunity to renew ourselves. In other words, it replenishes us. Loneliness is harsh, a deficiency state, a state of discontent marked by a sense of estrangement, an awareness of excess aloneness. Solitude is something you

165

choose. Loneliness is imposed on you by others ... Solitude gives us a chance to regain perspective. It renews us for the challenges of life ... Solitude restores body and mind. Loneliness depletes them.'[15]

Solitude for everyone, regardless of age, means we have to ignore the flotsam and jetsam that enter our thoughts. Solitude takes practice; however, it rests on a quiet confidence that, despite the immediate anxieties, all things shall be well. If we take the time to contemplate and to relish solitude we discover we are free to believe or not, because 'belief is not the final destination but only a form of support along the way'.[16] We will also find that we can rejoice in the freedom of non-achieving, we will also find there is a place beyond praise and beyond blame and guilt, and through this journey of contemplation and solitude we may discover, as Jesus suggests, that the Kingdom of Heaven is within.

Responsibility and forgiveness

'I have heard many stories about parents who have hurt their children so much, planting many seeds of suffering in them. But I believe that the parents did not mean to plant those seeds. They did not intend to make their children suffer. Maybe they received the same kinds of seeds from their parents. There is a continuation in the transmission of seeds, and their father and mother might have got those seeds from their grandfather and grandmother. Most of us are victims of a kind of living that is not mindful, and the practice of mindful living, of meditation, can stop these kinds of suffering and end the transmission of such sorrow to our children and grandchildren. We can break the cycle by not allowing these kinds of seeds of suffering to be transmitted to our children, our friends or anyone else.'[17]

The practice of gratitude provides the nursery slopes for such contemplative ageing, and for countering the inclination to ruminate. The significance of gratitude in relation to emotional wellbeing is one of the discoveries of positive psychology, although I recall my Sunday School teacher, Miss Venables back home in Bootle, likewise encouraged us to count our blessings and name them one by one. Gratitude or gratefulness 'is a knowing awareness that we are recipients of goodness,' writes Robert Emmons. He goes on to note that an 'essential aspect of gratitude is the notion of *undeserved merit*.'[18] If we habitually judge our lives against the lives of others, we squander the possibility of gratitude and we heighten the likelihood of being trapped in ruminating. Gratitude transforms our ruminating or miserable self, because it requires us to acknowledge the gift or generosity that comes from others, and encourages us to look outside ourselves.

Gratitude is one of the classical sources of human strength, along with wisdom, hope, love, spirituality and humility. The practice of gratitude is like grammar, in that it provides an underlying structure that helps us construct and make sense of our lives. Gratitude involves both reflection and action: acknowledgement of goodness in one's life and recognizing the source of this goodness, and the action of directing thanks outward. Gratitude, therefore, is more than a feeling because it requires an active response. To learn the grammar of gratitude, practise saying 'thank you' for happy *and* challenging experiences, for people, animals, things, art, memories, dreams. Saying thank you is more than just manners.

The power of thank you

'If the only prayer you ever say in your entire life is thank you, it will be enough.'

Meister Eckhardt

Realistically there will be times when circumstances are so hard that gratitude seems impossible. When alongside people confronted by harsh circumstances, the positive psychologists seem unembarrassed by drawing on religious practices. Emmons writes:

'The religious traditions encourage us to do more than react with passivity and resignation to a loss or crisis; they advise us to change our perspective, so that our suffering is transformed into an opportunity for growth.'[19]

Emmons amplifies how this comes about:

'Religious traditions ... articulate visions of how we should respond to the fact that life is full of suffering... People can adopt an attitude towards their suffering that allows it to be a meaningful component of life, perhaps opening the threshold to a deeper, more authentic existence.'[20]

By allowing existence itself to be a gift and ourselves to be enfolded in the grace or generosity of God, especially in trying times, the commitment to keep praising God is an act of defiance as well as an expression of gratitude. Baby boomers are often characterized by defiance, so we shall need to direct this attribute carefully if we are to be a boon to future generations, and not a pain in the butt.

Giving and receiving

This aim of turning the pattern of advantage away from ourselves towards younger and future generations as we approach later life gets fulsome encouragement from the grand-daddy of lifespan psychology – Erik Erikson. According to Erikson, as we become old we gain the capacity for what he refers to as 'grand-generativity'. He uses the term 'generativity' to describe middle age, with its responsibility for maintaining and perpetuating one's own household. His addition of the adjective 'grand' to this notion of generativity incorporates care of the present with concern for the future, especially for the future of younger generations and their futures, *and* for generations not yet born, *and* for the survival of the world as a whole. He writes that grand generativity:

'Contributes to the sense of immortality that becomes so important in the individual's struggle to transcend realistic despair as the end of life approaches, inevitably. However, grand-generative concern for the future in the abstract must be integrated with simple, direct caring for the specific individuals who are part of life today.'[21]

Erikson and his research colleagues provide the following example from their interviews of what is meant by this:

'For the past 10 years, one woman has housed Asian students for the International House at a local college. By now she has what she regards as a large international family of *grandchildren. Initially, she felt primarily that she was in a position to offer a service to these lonely foreigners. She was somewhat surprised at the warmth and closeness of the relationships she found herself developing with these strangers. Far from simply providing a room, she was providing a home and a family. To her surprise, they were providing her with a family in return. She came to enjoy the bustle they and their friends created in the kitchen. She liked stocking the refrigerator with soda and beer. She valued this renewed connection with college life. She loved hearing stories of their home countries. She was touched by their concern for her – by how they would look for things around the house that needed fixing or improving; would insist on accompanying her if she wanted to go out at night. With these students, this woman is able to enjoy caring and being cared for, free of the parental responsibilities and the years of personal history that may complicate generativity between parents and children.*[22]

If we are to embrace Erikson's challenge of 'grand generativity', then we owe it to younger and future generations to expose bogus routes to wellbeing, and we have to articulate this by our actions and habits as well as through our wise words. We know there is a mysterious riddle at the heart of happiness:

'Happiness comes from spiritual wealth, not material wealth... Happiness comes from giving, not getting. If we try hard to bring happiness to others, we cannot stop it from coming to us also. To get joy, we must give it, and to keep joy, we must scatter it'.[23]

If we haven't stopped consuming yet, or joking about our intention to spend the kid's inheritance, then we baby boomers need to act fast. It is not just the financial wealth of future generations that is affected; such a mindset fixed on the pursuit of pleasure and getting more stuff adds to the likelihood of our children and grandchildren buying into a deceitful prospectus. It is not just our rate of consumption[24] that we need to check if we are to pay our proper dues; we must also get a handle on our unhealthy narcissism, both for our own sake and for the sake of the future.

As well as demonstrating the possibility of stepping out of the tacky clutches of materialism, we have to demonstrate the possibility of rising above self-preoccupation. Baby boomers have been encircled by a narcissistic culture longer than any other generation, although upcoming generations have been enveloped *only* in a culture that fosters 'narcissistic greed'.[25] Ageing and death are considered to be the ultimate narcissistic wound from which there is no recovery. The person thus afflicted, like Narcissus in Ovid's tale, pines away locked in enduring and deep disappointment. To live one's final years in such a state is sad for the individual, but it is also a desultory, life-denying inheritance to bequeath to younger generations, as they witness such existential meaninglessness and passive – or more likely angry – disappointment.

Although it is not fashionable to say so, religion does wonders for bringing an over-vaunted view of the self down to the ground. All of us, contaminated by a narcissistic culture, face the choice of continuing to live with ever greater defendedness against the inevitability of ageing and death, or embracing the possibility of eternity in which one is, through grace, granted a place. Spiritual practice melts the hard-heartedness and self-preoccupation of narcissism and what may start off as a selfish pursuit of bliss, or holistic renewal will inevitably be transformed:

'Even though we may have embarked on the spiritual journey for purely narcissistic reasons, such as the search for bliss or relaxation, we find that things are not quite as we had planned once the journey gets underway. In spite of ourselves, and regardless of our motives, we find ourselves having to deal with realities that are not pleasant to the ego.'[26]

Despite our clear intentions, pursuit of the holy, or the sacred, changes us. It brings an 'about turn' or what in Christian terms is described as metanoia or conversion.

Tacey, in support of this transforming capacity of spirituality, notes the insistence of Buddhist teachers who declare that even a spiritual journey begun with impure motives, such as the search for personal power, can actually serve a greater purpose, and can become transformed into an authentic spiritual quest. The well-preened egos of a narcissistic culture misread the potency of spiritual practice and its capacity to call one out of one's self in response to a sense of 'otherness' and connectedness. Tacey concludes that an encounter with the holy:

'calls us to break our addiction to bliss, and to attend to the needs of the other... Once released from its hiding place in the self, it rushes out to the wider world, and we need to move beyond ourselves with it, lest we lose the gift of grace that has been bestowed on us.'[27]

Spiritual practices draw us out of ourselves and moisten the heart and this provides the urge towards compassion and ultimately towards action. This movement between inner and outer concerns is a characteristic of the established or formal religions, and explains the strong association between religious practice and active social responsibility. The expression of compassion becomes an expression of our *better self* and this provides the route through the perils of stagnation (Erikson's word) that perpetually plague us as we get older. Even though the struggle to discipline our tongue, restrain our temper and behave kindly to those nearest to us may get ever keener as we get older, the battle has to be fought if we are to bequeath to younger generations the hope that narcissism does not have to have the last word.

Notes

1. E. Howker and S. Malik (2010) *The Jilted Generation*, London: Icon Books p.152.
2. Ibid. p.156.
3. Ibid. p.163.
4. Dick Morris interviewed by Adam Curtis in 'The Century of the Self', part 4, BBC2, 7 April 2002 cited in E. Howker and S. Malik (2010) op. cit. p.183.
5. These references to Philippe Legrande's thoughts on a Land Value Tax are drawn from his article 'Tax the ground they walk on' in *Prospect* April 2010 and 'Tax land or carbon emissions but not hard work' in the *Financial Times* 9 April 2010.
6. In fact, Vince Cable did make a reference to a Land Value Tax in his speech to the Liberal Democrat Conference in September 2010: 'It will be said that in a world of internationally mobile capital and people it is counterproductive to tax personal income and corporate profit to uncompetitive levels. That is right. But a progressive alternative is to shift the tax base to property and land, which cannot run away, and represents in Britain an extreme concentration of wealth.'
7. Richard Reeves, comment made as part of the article 'Balancing the Books' in *Prospect* April 2010 p. 43.
8. See R. S Wilson and K. R. Krueger 'Loneliness and the Risk of Alzheimer's disease', *Archives of General Psychiatry* 64 (2007); 234 – 240.

9. J. T. Cacioppo and W. Patrick (2008) *Loneliness*, New York: W. W. Norton.
10. Phillip Larkin in a letter to his lover, Monica Jones 9 October 1952, 'Dearest Bun, I Didn't Want to Hurt You …' Compiled by A. Thwaite, published in the *Daily Telegraph Review* Saturday 2 October 2010.
11. P. Laslett (1989) *A Fresh Map of Life*, London: Weidenfeld and Nicolson p.134.
12. Ibid. p.1.
13. Mary Wolfe, 'Conversation' in L. D. Richardson and M. Wolfe (2001) *Principles and Practice of Informal Education*, London: Routledge Falmer p.130.
14. J. Strauss, T. Muday, K. McNall, & M. Wong (1997). 'Response Style Theory revisited: Gender differences and stereotypes in rumination and distraction', *Sex Roles*, 36, 771–92.
15. Hara Estroff Marano, 'What is Solitude' in *Psychology Today* July 2003, http://www.psychologytoday.com/articles/200308/what-is-solitude.
16. E. Sherman (2010) *Contemplative Aging*, New York: Gordian Knot Books p.164.
17. Thich Nhat Hanh, (1991) *Peace is Every Step*, New York: Bantam p.70.
18. R. Emmons (2007) *Thanks!*, New York: Houghton Mifflin Co. pp. 6–7 italics in the original.
19. Ibid p. 160.
20. Ibid p. 160.
21. E. H. Erikson, J. M. Erikson and H. Q. Kivnick, *Vital Involvement in Old Age*, (1986) New York Norton, adapted from p. 74–5 and p.93.
22. Ibid. p.99–100.
23. J. Templeton, unknown source, cited at http://www.worldofquotes.com/author/John-Templeton/1/index.html+%22John+Templeton%22+happiness.
24. UK baby boomers schooled in a traditional curriculum will know that 'consumption' referred to in the literature of the Restoration period and the eighteenth century was tuberculosis. It was referred to as consumption because it seemed to consume people from within. It is mysterious that this same term should be used to describe what we do with our spare cash.
25. The term 'narcissistic greed' was coined by Rob Mawdsley, 'Narcissism, Individuation and old Age' in *Narcissism - A Critical Reader*, eds, A. Gaitanidis and P. Curk (2007) London: Karnac p.175.
26. D. Tacey, *The Spirituality Revolution* (2004) Hove: Routledge p.147.
27. Ibid. p.147.

CHAPTER TEN

Old people ... don't make me laugh

This and the following chapter have a change of tone. They are altogether bleaker than what has gone before. In the following chapter I reflect on the dynamic of resentment and how this has to be taken into account when responding to the issue of intergenerational fairness. In this chapter I prepare the ground by considering the low value assigned to older people in western societies and the implications this has. As our societies age, and these same societies habitually ascribe low value to the aged, there are pitfalls to watch out for. In particular this chapter considers the advent of assisted dying and the hazards that are strewn along the way.

I wish I did not have to open this chapter with the word *valorization*, because as well as being an ugly word it is scarcely adequate to carry its important meaning. A dictionary might define valorization as an aspect of commerce, i.e. the amount of money that a thing is worth. Valorization also carries the idea of giving validity to something, but more even than this, valorization implies that the assigning of value and validity is determined externally, i.e. it is imposed from outside by the 'workings of market-like mechanisms'.[1] The word valorization means all these things, and valorization impacts on all stages of the lifespan.

An example of the impact of valorization is the treatment of girl babies in nations such as India, Nigeria, China and Pakistan, and sadly this is to name just a few of the nations where girls are assigned a low value. The *Times of India*, noting the fact that demography exposes acts carried on in private, observes that despite the anticipated equal number of births of boys and girls:

'In India the average is 927 girls for 1,000 boys ...even worse than countries like strife-racked Nigeria (965) and neighbouring Pakistan (958)... only China with 832 girls per 1,000 boys ranks below India on this dubious front... the dismal state of affairs is largely due to misuse of pre-natal diagnostic techniques ... the incidence of female foeticide seems more prevalent in urban areas... In Punjab, the number of girls in rural areas is 799 per 1000 boys, compared with an even grimmer 796 in urban zones.'[2]

I use this distressing information to illustrate 'the working of market-like mechanisms' that are a critical aspect of valorization. Think of the new mum in China or India on giving birth relief is likely to be palpable, perhaps immediately followed by the desire to hold and treasure the newborn babe, but on the discovery that the babe is a girl, deep affection has to be chased away and replaced by a sense of disappointment and possibly anxiety. But where does that disappointment and anxiety come from? It is generated by a source external to the mother, but so easily the destructive dynamic is internalized. History, even if in this case it is fictionalized history, provides an illustration of how valuing and devaluing gets internalized. Hilary Mantel in *Wolf Hall* puts these words into King Henry's mouth as he comes to terms with Anne Boleyn, his second wife, giving birth to a girl child, the Princess Elizabeth: 'Poor scrap. Her own mother will wish her away.'[3]

Valorization creeps into the fissure between perception and interpretation. Perception and interpretation are not the same thing. Between our seeing and our making sense of what we have seen or experienced is a complex and even mysterious *external* which has an impact within a split second. In the many lectures I have given on the issue of ageing I often tease my listeners with this quotation from Paul W Pruyser: 'Life views are shaped by a regnant gestalt of low-high-low proportions, an iconic illusion that pre-sorts all perceptions of the life course into a triphasic sequence.'[4] By the time I have completed the sentence a groan has usually risen from the audience. I risk this groan because this sentence from Pruyser gives some clues about the nanosecond gap between perception and interpretation. And more than this, Pruyser puts the spotlight on the way, in the fragment of a second, we assign value, or rather lack of value, to later life.

Pruyser uses the words 'ruling gestalt'; by this he means a pattern that we are so familiar with that when we see it, we experience a sense of completion or closure. A *gestalt* fills that nanosecond gap between seeing and interpreting. A ruling gestalt is a pattern that is so familiar that we shut down our critical faculties and automatically think we have *made sense* of what we have seen. Pruyser suggests that the dominant gestalt that imposes itself upon us in relation to the lifespan is that life consists of three phases. He adds:

'So much in the world proclaims a tripartite or triphasic pattern that we come to think of this pattern as a cosmic, ordained reality, and a *leitmotif* of life... thwart(ing) us from seeing, or making, alternative patterns.'[5]

However, as Pruyser emphasizes, these three phases are not valued equally in our own minds or by the wider world. The pinnacle of life is in the middle, and this assumption runs deep within our psyche and thereby assigns ageing to a relentless downward slope towards decrepitude and death.

Prior to the twentieth century, when people's lifespan was likely to be much shorter, one only had to live with the idea that one was on a relentless downward slope for a decade or perhaps fifteen years. Today, with increased longevity, despite cries that sixty is the new forty, the aged human being has to negotiate the slope to decrepitude for thirty years or more. This is a very long time to have to fight against negativity and devaluing, and such a drawn out battle of resistance inevitably takes its toll on one's self-image and the way in which one presents oneself to others.

An alliance with death and destruction?

Wolf Wolfensberger pioneered policies and practice to counter the negative valorization of groups of people. His focus has been particularly on the way in which people with disabilities are devalued, and he promoted the policy and practice of normalization, especially for people with learning difficulties.[6] However, Wolfensberger suggests that society doesn't just devalue certain groups, it has deep seated destructive intentions towards these groups, but these destructive and unpleasant urges are denied and repressed into our collective unconscious.

Wolfensberger was scorned because of his emphasis on society as some kind of cognate being, (in this context 'cognate' means having the same root and therefore the same nature and inclination), and particularly his perception that this cognate entity called society:

'has made an identity alliance with death and ... working feverishly towards the destruction of life on this planet ... in a very well hidden policy of genocidal destruction of certain of its rejected and unwanted classes ... Once a society has made a decision ... it will transact this decision through whatever technical measures it may take towards this group, even those measures that are interpreted as being to the (devalued group's) benefit.'[7]

This kind of grand theorizing has won Wolfensberger few friends but many enemies. Few of Wolfensberger's critics consider they need to defend aborting a foetus that shows signs of abnormality, because it seems such an obviously sensible thing to do, a situation which Wolfensberger would consider evidence of the cognate destructive drive that he postulates. However, the main critique of Wolfensberger's thinking comes from those concerned with woman's rights, who especially take umbrage with his view that the massive haemorrhage of life through abortion is also an example of the 'alliance with death and destruction' that he postulates.

Those who know their feminist theories will recognize that there is plenty of room for agreement between feminists and Wolfensberger's uncompromising assessment. Simone de Beauvoir, who is usually credited with opening the door to feminist thinking, argues, like Wolfensberger, that society has the capacity to act as a corporate entity, and this unconscious (and sometimes conscious) dynamic has enveloped women in mystery and served to place women into a category that is beyond understanding, recognition or help. Like Wolfensberger, de Beauvoir, regardless of objections, took her argument further to suggest that stereotyping is visited upon the less powerful by the more powerful as a means of protecting the interests of the powerful.[8] Andrea Dworkin, also a feminist writer, urges us, like Wolfensberger, to take seriously the role that images have in devaluing groups. For Dworkin, pornographic images of women betray a deeper intent, creating a climate in which acts of degradation, carelessness and even brutality become acceptable.[9]

It is not just images of lithesome women that objectify and devalue. Age and ageing are also the subject of derogatory images. Ironically many of these negative images are used by agencies that seek to support older people. Countless images of frail and troubled elderly people, usually women, are used as a means of prising money out of potential donors; and ipso facto, the dynamic of valorization is so effective that to be in receipt of charity is to be cast immediately into a socially devalued or pathetic role.

Get used to being laughed at

Humour is also used to devalue older people, and baby boomers will by now be familiar with receiving birthday cards that carry some kind of derogatory message about the number of candles required on the birthday cake, or parts of the anatomy that sag, or wrinkles that might pass as a road map. Mostly we think that jokes are harmless, and for sure the world would be a more miserable place if humour ceased to break through. However, humour does carry a cost, and that cost is usually carried by the more vulnerable, or those least welcome at the party: mothers-in-law and Liverpudlians remain acceptable targets, and in a pre-politically correct era the list also included Irish people and other ethnic minorities.

As long ago as 1954 Allport, in his ground breaking book *The Nature of Prejudice*,[10] noted how jokes enable derogatory views to enter the public domain and provide a foundation for more serious expressions of prejudice. He coined the term 'antilocution' to describe this potent brew that involves belittling others, confirming stereotypes *and* gaining an accolade for having brought laughter to one's listeners. Allport, on the basis of research among refugees in the Second World War, compiled a worryingly short scale between laughter and extermination – yes, extermination. The scales begins with:

... 'antilocution' – e.g. telling jokes...
... leading to avoidance ...
... leading to devaluing and discrimination ...
... leading to physical attack – or neglect ...
... ending up with extermination.

This scale devised by Allport may look extreme and exaggerated, but the following three cartoons suggest that something menacing lurks not too far below the surface. They are far from exceptional: they come from the *Church Times*, a birthday card and from *Private Eye*. It would be easy to provide a host of other examples. First let me admit to having laughed at all three, despite all three suggesting that it is acceptable to kill or maim old people. I focus on just one of them: the 'Desperate Dan' character depicted in the cartoon from *Private Eye*. The cartoon appeared in 1987, this was when marketing executives had coined the use of the heart sign ♥ to launch a series of advertising campaigns, ranging from 'I ♥ New York', 'I ♥ my (Mini) Metro' and even Glasgow got in the act with 'I ♥ Glasgow'. However, closer scrutiny of the symbol on the chest of the 'Desperate Dan' figure suggests his intent was not on loving his granny but clubbing her. Yes, I confess to having laughed in both instances.[11]

181

As I contemplated this cartoon and the ease with which I laughed, I pondered on whether there was any other category of life on earth, other than grannies, that could have been depicted in this way. I thought of 'I ♣ seal pups' but decided that would be distasteful rather than funny. I then thought of

"Have you had the batteries out of your grandad's pacemaker?"

ethnic groups and swiftly moved on, because I had suddenly hit that penultimate stage identified by Allport: physical attack and then … extermination. So why, in our cognate society, is it acceptable to laugh about clubbing grannies? Why had grannies escaped the censure of political correctness?

It was this cartoon from *Private Eye* that prompted my interest in ageing.[12] It did this because I have enough social scientific knowledge to know that sometimes humour and laughter can betray us and expose powerful, unresolved emotions. The reason for this is rooted in psychoanalysis and its interest in repression and unconscious desires. The notion is that material which is repressed can sometimes surface in

St Gargoyle's

Terry hadn't done a funeral since February

bizarre ways, laughter being a prime example. The cartoon that invited me to laugh at the idea of grannies being clubbed, provided a clue that the issue of ageing would yield a host of insights if only it was subjected to honest and imaginative thinking.

In addition to some forms of laughter, the other example that gets cited as an expression of the bizarre return of repressed emotions is the extent to which entertainment focuses on death, which of course is a close cousin of ageing. A good night out at the cinema, or watching the TV, or computer gaming are all likely involve many if not a multitude of deaths. Only sedate films and TV serials resist the temptation to dramatize death and depict cadavers, perhaps for this reason they tend to be the favourites of grannies.

To summarize so far

The dynamic of valorization impacts on everyone: no one is spared, not even Jesus; just consider his evaluation of the Canaanite woman, whom he at first dismissed because she was an Arab and therefore unworthy compared to his fellow Jews.[13] *The experience of being treated as someone of low value very easily gets internalized, so that the person or group of people take on the view of themselves as in some way deficient.*

Pruyser coined the expression 'regnant gestalt' to emphasize how we are inclined to see the world in terms of patterns, and when we have recognized a familiar pattern, a sense of completion follows speedily. Pruyser suggested that we see the life stages as holding to a distinctive pattern – an upward slope towards middle age, and then, after a period, old age dawns and this third, old age stage is characterized by a downward slope. Pruyser suggests that this view of ageing dominates our perceptions to the extent that we internalize this idea and continually have this deficit view of old age reinforced by the wider culture and society.

Next we turned to Wolf Wolfensberger, who pioneered efforts to counter this process of devaluing. He makes a powerful claim: he suggests that devaluing people is only the tip of the iceberg; lurking underneath is a dastardly, repressed 'death wish' that, ultimately, he suggests will lead to 'rejected and unwanted classes' not just being excluded but becoming the focus of death-dealing.

We then looked at laughter and jokes, suggesting that jokes and cartoons may not always be benign because they can give energy to prejudice. Allport suggests that 'antilocution', his label for telling jokes that demean and mock, is only four steps away from the extermination of those whom the joke or cartoon has made vulnerable. The fact that jokes and cartoons about older people are all around and mysteriously avoid the censoring of political correctness, should make us smell a rat.

Dastardliness and the right to die

I have tried to use the word 'dastardly' with some precision. Dastardly means sneaky, sly or devious and deceitful. And in this case the deceit and sneakiness is so deep that it is hard to know how to counter it. However, traditional societies, particularly in African and Indo-Pacific cultures, have developed a means of protecting the aged from such dastardly intent by evolving the idea that the dead have power over the living. Those closest to death are therefore closest to the achievement of supernatural power which can be used for good or for ill. Therefore, those alongside the frail aged and soon to be departed have good reason to be generous and gentle in their dealings.

In the West, we rely on the law to provide protection. However, there is now pressure to change the law to permit assisted dying to help end a person's life, should the person perceive the burden of pain and distress to be beyond their capacity. This request for assistance is a logical extension of a person's right to choose, and the 'right to choose' is a powerful mantra in a culture dominated by a market economy that aims to deliver what we want. However, the insights from commentators such as Wolfensberger, Pruyser and Allport suggest that people (that is, you and I!), are likely to be compromised in their judgements because of the dastardliness of the implicit, and sometimes explicit, attitude of the wider society which provides the backdrop to growing older and older. Too easily we take on board, or internalize, the devaluing practices of those around us and our wider culture.

This propensity to absorb the negativity projected from the wider society has to be taken seriously in the debate about helping people to die. For example, Pruyser, in postulating the notion of a 'regnant gestalt' (ruling pattern), suggests we buy into the idea that once we enter the decades of later life we face an inevitable downhill and downbeat journey, and we feel that this is so natural that we have a sense of completion and feel at home with the idea. Add to this the acceptability and pervasiveness of older people being the butt of jokes and cartoons that belittle and undermine, then extreme caution must be exercised about opening up a legal route to assisted suicide/euthanasia.

A Grimm's Fairytale

Once upon a time the people of a remote mountain village used to sacrifice and eat their old men. A day came when there was not a single old man left, and the traditions were lost. They wanted to build the great house for the meetings of the assembly, but when they came to look at the tree-trunks that had been cut for that purpose no one could tell the top from the bottom: if the timbers were placed the wrong way up it would set up a series of disasters. A young man said that if they promised never to eat the old men any more, he would be able to find a solution. They promised. He brought his grandfather, whom he had hidden; and the old man taught the community to tell the top from the bottom.[14]

In a society where a person's right to choose is paramount, it becomes hard to resist the right of an older person, assumed to be in their right mind, to express their desire for euthanasia. However, the case is being made here that there is sufficient analysis, if not actual evidence, to suggest that as older people we are scarcely ever likely to be in our right minds in relation to the ending of our lives. Friedrich Engels used the expression 'false consciousness' to describe how the workers (or 'proletariat' to use his and his friend Karl Marx's terminology) are misguided as to their true desires and wants, and have to struggle to comprehend what is in their true interests. Such revolutionary meanderings may not appeal, but insights, from whatever source, need to be harnessed in the light of the dismal prediction by Wolfensberger, that 'Once a society has made a decision ... it will transact this decision through whatever technical measures it may take towards this group, even those measures that are interpreted as being to the (devalued group's) benefit.'[15] One would hope that Wolfensberger is wrong, but there is just a possibility that he is alerting us to some dastardly truth about human nature.

For older people, as well as unconscious or deep seated drives, there are also *conscious* drives to take into account. Simone de Beauvoir, after her intricate analysis of the many dimensions of ageing, concludes that, 'The vast majority of mankind looks upon the coming of old age with sorrow or rebellion. It fills them with more aversion than death itself.'[16] There is a basic reason why old age is a more menacing prospect than death: it is because we cannot imagine a state that is beyond our existence, but we can imagine only too well the pains and distresses of old age. Florida Scott Maxwell, in her remarkable exploration of her own experience of growing old, writes:

'We wonder how much older we have to become, and what degree of decay we may have to endure. We keep whispering to ourselves, "Is this age yet? How much further must I go?" For age can be dreaded more than death...It is waiting for death that wears us down, and the distaste for what we may become.'[17]

To this dread of the pains and perils that may befall us is to be added the awareness that to stay alive requires a disproportionate share of limited resources. This awareness is particularly heightened if we baby boomers seek to be a pivot generation, endeavouring to re-balance the distribution of resources between generations. However, caution is needed because this feeling of living too long, and using up medical resources, can have its roots in cultural bullying. By this I mean a dominant cultural perspective that sets our perceptions of ourselves and of our obligations on a debasing route.

For the current old generation, often surprised by the assets accumulated through a lifetime that began in hard times, the thought must surface that they sit on wealth from which younger generations of the family could benefit. In particular, for those who move into residential care, the sense of using up hard-won resources can be intense. Awareness of the weekly cost of staying in a care home, combined with awareness of how rapidly one's assets can be used up, is debilitating. Assets, that may for decades have been marshalled for the benefit of children and grandchildren, disappear at such a rate that the frail older person cannot help but wish they could be dead.

For younger 'old' generations, such as the baby boomers, our thoughts may focus on the fear that we will prove lacking in relation to the resilience and courage needed to cope with the challenges of future frailty. The chances are that we, like the very old, will also have imbibed the idea that the nature of the care available to us as we become frail is to be dreaded more than death itself. We may have journeyed alongside the mentally frail, and found ourselves secretly wishing that death would come and befriend swiftly, rather than inching its way along. This fear of prolonged suffering, because of the slowness to die from the various forms of dementia or from recurrent medical interventions, may upgrade the possibility of helping someone to die to a secular sacrament.

> For I am already being poured out like a drink offering, and the time has come for my departure. I fought the good fight, I have finished the race, I have kept the faith.[18]
>
> St Paul writing to Timothy

Scanning the horizon

From where I sit, weighing the pressures rather than the pros and cons for assisted dying, I conclude that the generation anticipating old age will want to be spared the challenges of senility, and there is no force in the land that will be able to resist the call to be spared the end-of-life struggle. Legalization approving aid-in-dying seems inevitable. However, it does not nullify two substantial fears:

- Older people, especially frail older people, risk self-deprecation to an extent that the perception of their worth is so low that poise collapses, and negativity hastens the loss of the will to live.
- The dastardliness that dogs our collective enterprise will welcome and embrace such inclinations and will be

'relaxed' about monitoring and publicizing the number of people seeking interventions to hasten the end of life.

Having offered such an intense and worrying assessment, it would be cowardly to back away from suggesting some responses to this very personal and public predicament. The first suggestion is that we shift terminology away from talk of assisted suicide. This term has developed to protect any third party who may have helped someone to end their life. A better description would be 'assisted death' or 'assisted dying'.

The challenge will also be in relation to how assisted death is to be provided. Is it to be in the hands of the GP? But then immediately the shadow of Dr Shipman looms. Is it something that is administered on hospital wards, or in some peaceful location by those opting to perform such intervention? The suggestion made here is that assisted dying should be added to the repertoire of palliative care specialists. Palliative care has been one of the boons of the last forty years. The skill of supporting people as they or their loved ones approach death has become a recognized specialism, and the hospices that have grown up around the country receive exceptional community support. Hospices are one of the few places where a relationship of any depth is possible between doctor and patient. In no other context do we dare risk allowing the potent development of 'assisted dying' to take root. However, the likelihood is that because most hospices are independent charities, many with a Christian foundation, there will be many hospices that decline to offer assistance towards death.

Palliative care is associated with care for those with cancer and other terminal diagnoses. Hospices as we know them are not a viable environment for those with dementia, and mostly the provision for those with dementia is very much meaner and less sympathetic than the provision made for those with more obvious terminal illnesses. It is in relation to dementia where the greatest moral alertness is needed, because the person cloaked by dementia is least able to speak for themselves. In fact, the plight of those with dementia is so merciless that the condition of dementia confounds the standard definition of euthanasia: 'The deliberate termination of a person's life, normally upon the wish of the person who dies.'[19] The implication of this is that those with dementia or severe stroke illness face the dreadful slow fading associated with 'passive euthanasia'[20] – and so too their loved ones take part in this slow and solemn journey. If help in dying is to become part of the repertoire of palliative care, then serious efforts have to be made to extend the sensitive and responsive care that is associated with hospices to those who struggle with the slow, slow death associated with the dementias.

Debate about assisted dying is not solely linked to the aged. In fact research in the Netherlands suggests that physician-assisted suicides are particularly high for those aged between 25 and 44 years, and lowest among those aged 80 or more.[21] But this research was conducted in 1997, a time of economic growth rather than a time of straightened circumstances, when talk about rationing resources escalates. This economic fact betrays the harshness that lurks very close to discussion about assisted dying. Times of shortage lead to increased compe-tition for scarce resources and the potentially conflicting needs of older and younger age groups come to the fore. This heightens the danger of those with cognitive impairment being assigned to the category of 'non-treatment' and left to wither with minimal care. We have to face up to this reality, and only when we have done this should we wager an opinion on the rights and wrongs of being helped to die.

This reflection on the place of assisted dying comes to a conclusion: that the desire for assisted dying is strong and multidirectional and therefore inevitable. However, the arguments in favour of the acceptance of assisted dying are not always trustworthy, particularly the argument that 'It's my right to choose'. In reality, the case for assisted dying has been won and no arguments to the contrary will be able to prevail. The reason for the delay in bringing forward legislation is rooted in the complexity of the legal drafting and the reluctance of politicians to go down in history as the movers of such significant and death-dealing proposals. This shifts the challenge away from resisting legislation towards ensuring every effort is made to resist the susceptibility of the vulnerable to the dastardliness that is part of our human nature. To do this means that we have to develop confidence in what counts as a good death, and this is a major challenge in a secular and individualized society.

A good death

A good birth and a good death have many things in common, so notes John Vincent. We would wish both to be:

- timely
- wanted
- fulfilling
- free from complications
- enfolded within precious relationships[22]

These characteristics help to locate the potential contribution of assisted dying to a good death, providing criteria that all involved can engage with and exercise some judgement, although, as with childbirth, the view of the medics will carry more weight than anyone else's. However, these five feature are drawn from a secular and individualistic reference point, and this provides niggardly sustenance for what is the 'last achievement'.[23] Just as childbirth is an achievement, so too the idea of death being an achievement is apt.

It was just his time

In Swaziland I stayed with a medical assistant of the government clinic. His father was also staying with him. His father was a gentle, happy man in his late 60s, who lived 80 miles away. On my next monthly round I was shocked to be told by my friend that his father had just died at the family home. I expressed surprise, since he had seemed to be in excellent health, and asked of what he had died. 'Nothing, it was just his time. We have four children in the family, so he came to stay with each of us for a week and talk and play with all the grandchildren, and to say goodbye. He reached home last week, and now he has gone. It is good.'

Donald Arden, in comparing this experience with practice in the West, writes: 'It is indeed good, and better than our complex way of prolonging life in order to launch ourselves on disputations about the rightness of shortening it again to its natural span.'[24]

Ladislaus Boros, in his book *The Moment of Truth*, speaks of dying as the event which gives man (sic) the opportunity of posing his first completely personal act.[25] This description of the act of dying highlights the inherent loneliness that is involved, and again the inherent loneliness of childbirth continues the parallel between birth and death. However, the parallels break down when we consider the attention that is given to the challenge of childbirth compared to the preparation for death. Death, like birth, is part of the human condition and we have to find a way of dealing with it, but in comparison with childbirth little attention is given to this non-negotiable experience that confronts each of us. Death presents a huge problem to a secular society. In the absence of the 'big' stories about the meaning of life (the grand narratives), it is difficult to express the purpose and meaning of life. This means talk of death elides into recognition that there is nothing to live for, and such public discourse is too dangerous to encourage.

In a culture which has moved ever closer to extreme individualism and lost confidence in religion, it is difficult to give meaning to death. John Vincent puts it this way: 'Our culture of extreme individualism isolates people from collective meaning systems and responses to death. For a society in which individuality is the supreme virtue, 'ashes to ashes, dust to dust' is a message without consolation.'[26] For those of us who take our faith seriously, our task is to remind our society of its almost forgotten memory of what it means to be human. The risk is that we baby boomers, in our negligent secularism, underestimate how vital, in the very sense of 'life giving', is a narrative that gives meaning to our lives.

What has been lost is recoverable

'In achieving material abundance we have begun to lose our moral and spiritual bearing. We have focused on the how but not the why. In achieving technical mastery we have lost sight of the question -- to what end? Valuing science at the expense of ethics, we have unparalleled knowledge of what is and unprecedented doubts about what ought to be. Luckily, all that we have lost is recoverable. We are not prisoners of time because we have the databanks of collective memory through which the past speaks to the present and guides it on its way. The human spirit is unique in its capacity to correct its own errors. What we damage, we can repair. What we destroy, we can rebuild. There is one proviso: that we do not lose our sense of hope'.[27]

In a secular world death is the point of utter separation and utter loneliness. In contrast, the Christian story gives meaning to this 'moment of truth', for it is the return of our life to the God who gave it, and although a deeply personal moment, it is not a lonely one, for Jesus has followed that same mysterious journey and made the way clear. There is a generosity to this companionship. By just holding the space open to the possibility of accompaniment into a new dawning, or the possibility of a new way of seeing, or the possibility of a vision of the true God, it dignifies the act of dying, making the ending also the arrival into newness for which we were created.

Hope is the gift that comes to the person of faith, and Christians are specific about the nature of this hope, for it is hope in the resurrection. However, perhaps this gift that comes with faith in Jesus is better described as trust. The problem with hope is that it ties everything to an outcome, and too easily the outcome becomes what really matters. Trust, on the other hand, describes our relationship to the actual process that is taking place. In our dying, and in trusting Jesus, perhaps we come upon Heaven. But even here Dante suggests we should not expect hope. Dante, in the Divine Comedy, when he finally arrives in Paradise after his long journey, hears the laughter of angels praising the Trinity. According to Dante, in Hell there is no hope and no laughter, in Purgatory there is hope but no laughter, but in Heaven there is no need of hope, so laughter reigns. Such laughter will not be at the expense of others but because of the release from a struggle well wrought.

Notes

1. J. O'Brien 'Nobody Outruns the Trickster: A Brief Note on the Meaning of the Word "Valorization"' in *SRV-VRS: The International Social Role Valorization Journal*, vol. 1 (2) 1994 pp. 34–5.
2. H. Dhawan 'Sex ratio keeps getting worse' the *Times of India*, December 10, 2006.
3. H. Mantel (2009) *Wolf Hall*, London: Fourth Estate p. 485.
4. P. W. Pruyser 'Aging: Downward, Upward, or Forward?' in *Pastoral Psychology*, Vol. 24 (229), Winter 1975 pp. 102–118. Quote from pp. 102–3.
5. Ibid p. 103.
6. Wolfensberger later changed his terminology, moving from 'normalisation' (which can easily imply that those who are devalued have to make the effort to become 'normal') to the term 'social role valorization'.
7. W. Wolfensberger (1987) 'Values in the funding of social services', *American Journal of Mental Deficiency* 92: 141–3 p.141.
8. S. de Beauvoir (1972) *The Second Sex*. See particularly Chapter 3 'Old Age in Historical Societies'.
9. H. Brown and H. Smith 'Assertion, not assimilation: A feminist perspective on the normalisation principle' in (eds) H. Brown and H. Smith (1992) *Normalization*, London: Routledge p. 151.
10. G. Allport (1954) *The Nature of Prejudice*, Reading MA: Addison-Wesley.
11. The fact that this cartoon requires the viewer to look twice (at least it did in 1987 when we were surrounded by all the heart-shaped advertisements) is an illustration of the impact of a 'regnant gestalt' referred to earlier when discussing Pruyser's insights.
12. At that time my interest was academic, whereas now it has become more personal.
13. The significance of this story in Matthew 15 and Mark 7 cannot be over-emphasized because it gives an exceptional insight into sin, and original sin in particular. It raises the possibility of the dynamic of 'valorization' as being an aspect of original sin, i.e. a plight that is part

and parcel of being human. The fact that Jesus gets caught up in valorization is an indication of just how human he was, and the struggle Jesus had was that of resisting the sin of sloth – letting some snake (as in the Garden of Eden) tell him what to think, for it is sloth, the refusal to think for ourselves that opens the door to the dynamic of valorization. Jesus allows himself to engage in dialogue with this woman and is given a gift – a new way of seeing. The fundamental shift the Arab woman wrought in Jesus was for him to recognize the inclusive nature of his ministry – that everyone was and is a child of God, and not just Jewish people.

14. S. de Beauvoir (1972) op. cit. p.77.
15. W. Wolfensberger (1987) op. cit. p.141.
16. S. de Beauvoir (1972) op. cit. p.539.
17. F. Scott Maxwell (1968) *The Measure of my Days*, New York: Alfred A. Knopf p. 138.
18. 2 Timothy vv. 6–7 (NIV).
19. J. Phillips, K. Ajrouch, and S. Hillcoat-Nalletamby (2010) *Key Concepts in Social Gerontology*, London:Sage p. 91.
20. Passive euthanasia implies the withdrawal of any kind of support that can sustain life and this includes the withdrawal of nourishment and liquids.
21. B. Onwuteaka-Philipson, M. Muller, and G. Van Der Wal (1997) 'Euthanasia and Old Age' in Age and Ageing, 26: pp. 487–492.
22. Based on John Vincent's analysis in *Old Age*, (2003) London: Routledge p.159–160.
23. This is the title of a book written by Willem Berger, a Dutch Roman Catholic Priest and psychologist. See W. Berger (1974) *The Last Achievement*, London: The Grail.
24. Based on D. S. Arden in *Anglican Theological Review*, Supplementary Series, June 1976, p.24.
25. L. Boros (1989)*The Moment of Truth (Mysterium Mortis)*, London: Burns and Oates.
26. J. Vincent (2003) *Old Age*, London: Routledge p.155.
27. J. Sacks (2000) *Celebrating Life*, London: Continuum p. 172–3.

CHAPTER ELEVEN

Resentment: The dastardly bushfire

The debate about intergenerational fairness, or extending justice into the future, whatever the title that is used, is highly volatile. Resentment is easily aroused, and resentment can have all the features of the dastardly bushfire described on the first page of this book. Like the bushfire, once started, resentment is very hard to put out. Like the bushfire, the growth of resentment is something we can foster or resist, but the danger of resentment never goes away. Finally, when it takes hold, resentment provides a springboard that adds momentum to unruly and uncivil developments. Resentment, like the bushfire, can trigger a dastardly progression of individual and social ills.

Once upon a time, old age was a protected category, protected from the public expression of resentment by the idea of worthiness or deservedness. Willingness to put oneself out for those whom we think are deserving, or those for whom we feel sorry, provided the basis for the contract between the generations. However, no longer is old age, or any category of humankind, allocated any special status or granted exceptional respect, because the aspiration is that everyone should be treated as an equal. The special category of being deserving or worthy, based on the accumulation of credits and contributions one may have made in the past, has been trumped by the principle of equal opportunities. The risk is that this loss of special status for older people creates a vacuum into which resentment can flow.

However, there is a distinctive way in which 'fairness' can be applied to old age. Age, unlike gender or ethnicity, is not a permanent characteristic attached to a person throughout life. Each of us, over time, will find ourselves ageing and becoming old, at least that is our hope. The very fact that we speak of the unfairness of someone dying young endorses this unique trait. However:

> 'When we are young or in our prime we do not think of ourselves as already being the dwelling place of our own future old age... If we do not know what we are going to be, we cannot know what we are: let us recognize ourselves in this old man or in that old woman. It must be done if we are to take upon ourselves the entirety of our human state.'[1]

Old age lies in wait for us all

When Buddha was still Prince Siddartha, he often escaped from the splendid palace in which his father kept him shut up and drove about the surrounding countryside. The first time he went out he saw a tottering, wrinkled, toothless, white-haired man, bowed, mumbling and trembling as he propped himself along on his stick. The sight astonished the Prince and his charioteer told him just what it meant to be old. 'It is the world's pity,' cried Siddartha, 'That weak and ignorant beings, drunk with the vanity of youth, do not behold old age! Let us hurry back to the palace. What is the use of pleasures and delights, since I myself am the future dwelling-place of old age?'[2]

This unique trait of old age that, barring misfortune, it is everyone's destiny, makes the resentment of older people a risky business, for it involves resentment of what we are to become. The inclination to accuse older generations of having messed up the future is dangerous for everyone, because in provoking resentment it risks leading younger generations[3] into a negative view of what it is to be old – and therefore a negative view of their future selves.

Blaming – doing what comes naturally

It is a particularly big ask for younger generations to resist the temptation to blame older people for their tough circumstances compared with the apparently easy blessings heaped upon older generations. The habit of blaming is thought of as acceptable logic, it is natural, common sense, akin to causation in science. So when problems arise we look for the *cause* that produced the *effect*, and from here confidently apportion blame. However, no problem can be seen in isolation, so the ease with which we drift into the assumption that such a person, or in this instance such a generation, is the cause of the problem wrenches apart the complex pattern of interrelationships that all play a part in *causation*. To use the jargon, the problem is in the whole, not the part, it is *the system that is the locus of the problem.*

Systems thinking aims to address the whole and examine the interrelationship between the parts. This is different from the usual form of analysis, which aims to take apart an event or issue into constituent parts (this is in fact the root meaning of the word *analysis*). Systems thinking means that, instead of isolating smaller and smaller parts, it widens and deepens our view of the issue and therefore takes into account more and more factors. There is a second aspect to take into account in relation to systems thinking: the interrelationship of the factors that are impacting on a situation are so closely intertwined that a change in relation to one factor has an impact throughout the system. This means that a change in one area reverberates throughout the system.

The work of Wilkinson and Pickett referred to in Chapter Four provides a good illustration of this mysterious interrelationship. Their research shows how the gap between rich and poor matters to both rich and poor: if the gap widens the wellbeing of both the poor *and* the rich falls. This intricate inter-relationship illustrates how my behaviour and the behaviour of everyone else is enfolded by the most complex of *feed back loops,* some of which may be immediate and others long term, but all of which play a part in the outcome. From this subtle, almost inexplicable interrelationship[4] comes a very down-to-earth insight: that we are all in it together. We are indeed our brother's and sister's keeper.

If, in relation to fairness between the generations, we opt to break down the issue into constituent parts, rather than appreciate that everything is connected to everything else, the resulting analysis will be simplistic and off-beam. For example we could blame women for going out to work, not having children, ending their marriages in divorce and causing the price of houses to rise. We could blame medical care for prolonging life at all costs; we could blame the Germans for the war and causing people to hold off having children and thus bringing a bulge in the birth rate when peace was secured. We could blame the baby boomers for developing a selfish set of values and keeping the best for themselves; we could blame capitalism for shaping our tastes and wrecking the planet, forgetting that capitalism and the markets on which capitalism relies implicate you and me. When we acknowledge that we are all part of the problem, then the inclination to *blame* is likely to fall away. By understanding system dynamics we can step outside of blaming, and free ourselves from the tyranny of there being an enemy or bogy man who is responsible for all our problems.[5]

Servant capitalism?

The extraordinary thing about capitalism is its humility and refusal to judge. It will give us what we want; it will not force on us what it thinks we need. Often, we are disgusted by what we discover we want – but that reflects on us, not on the servant that brings us our fetish gear and saturated fats. It could bring us organic turnips, just as happily.[6]

The inclination to look for someone or some group on which we can blame things, can prompt another dastardly progression. Once we get into the habit of blaming a specific group, especially when times are tough, anxiety and fear easily gain momentum, and before long we find ourselves behaving instinctively and scapegoating and, ultimately, death-dealing. Scapegoating, like antilocution, is the first step in the dastardly progression. Just as Allport suggests that jokes that belittle others (antilocution) enable derogatory views to enter the public domain, and subtly give licence to more serious expressions of prejudice[7] (see Chapter Ten), so, too, scapegoating leads to similarly nasty outcomes.

One person who writes powerfully about the seduction of scapegoating is René Girard. Girard wrote from the perspective of anthropology as well as from modern literature.[8] He begins his explanation of the dynamic of scapegoating by postulating the 'mimetic of desire', which is jealousy, but with a twist. We discover what we want by observing what others find desirable. In other words, our desires mimic what other people desire (hence Girard's use of the word 'mimetic'). Having 'caught' our desires from others, in a context of scarcity, more and more people begin to want what only some can have. This results in a struggle to obtain what we want, and can lead to a generalized antagonism towards the individual or group that seems to be responsible for the disappointment. These dynamics, identified by Girard, offer an extraordinarily apt description of the intergenerational dynamics that are developing between younger generations and the baby boom generation.

Girard suggests that the continued copying and desire for what others are seen to have involves the repeated raising of hopes, to be followed by disappointment, and from there a dastardly progress can gain momentum. Few can withstand hopes being repeatedly dashed and frustration is almost certain to result, which in turn gives energy and inclination to ganging together (herding) with others who are similarly disappointed and frustrated. From this point it is only a short step to trying to do down those who seem to be the cause of the frustration, and from here scapegoating can develop its own momentum. It can be a very fierce driver, to include the casting out those to whom blame is assigned.

Girard suggests that the vicious riddance of those who are blamed for frustration and discontent can temporarily reduce the desire for violence. However, if the action of casting out or casting aside does not result in a sense of fairness returning, then the assumption is that more scapegoats need to be sacrificed. Scapegoating those whom we blame because they seem to have prevented us getting what we want is a form of rough justice that has been a characteristic of the species since Day One, and is founded on cheap solidarity and cheap hope.

Girard provides a route out of this reactive inclination to blame and scapegoat and he does this through an anthropological and literary analysis of scapegoating in Judeo-Christian texts. Examining the Old (The Torah) and New Testaments, he traces how scapegoating was expressed in Old Testament times and then notes the extraordinary rejection of scapegoating in the New Testament. He notes Jesus' clear intention to move people beyond this habitual dastardly progression, for example:

- Jesus repeatedly teaches his followers that he is to be the *final* scapegoat.
- The Gospels' are written from the perspective of the scapegoat, the one who is blamed and who is put to death. The Gospels, Girard suggests, provide the first (and rare) example of literature that encourages people to see the world through the eyes of the scapegoat.
- The scapegoat in the Gospels rises again, triumphant, refusing to let the death of the scapegoat be the final act. Whether one takes this triumph over death as mythological, or as 'really real', is of little significance for Girard. His point is that the Gospels represent an enormous step forward in moving beyond the primitive urge to kill the scapegoat.

There is a further feature that Girard notes, and it concerns Jesus' wish that his followers should regularly re-enact the last supper, taking wine and bread to recall the death of the scapegoat (Mass means 'sacrifice'), and to give thanks (Eucharist means thanksgiving), because the scapegoat defies the dastardly progression of death-dealing by triumphing over the grave. The implication of this for Girard is that this regular re-enactment carries the potential to move the followers of Jesus beyond the habit of scapegoating.

Few churches or Christians seem to be aware of this explicit challenge to the habit of scapegoating and blaming that is uniquely articulated in the Gospels.[9] It is for this reason that it forms part of the five essentials of second chance theology described in Chapter Five. Resisting the temptation to blame and scapegoat is an essential discipline in negotiating the tricky times that are ahead. Christians have a special calling to resist the inclination to blame, as much as we have a special calling to exercise forgiveness and to seek forgiveness for our proclivity towards dastardliness. There is a timeliness associated with this distinctive resistance to scapegoating that Jesus enables; it is timely because in our narcissistic culture everyone is at fault or to blame – except for the over-vaunted self. Churches, in the light of this, perhaps need to focus more frequently on this aspect of the salvation that Jesus brings.

Love holds things together

Systems thinking has to be at the heart of Christian thinking. When St Paul is confronted by the quarrels and disputes in Corinth he offers the image of a body with many parts as a means of encouraging unity despite difference: 'As it is, there are many parts, but one body.'[10] Paul, having commended this systems approach in which the parts and whole are intricately interrelated, then goes on to write one of the most inspiring passages in any of his many letters: 'And now I will show you the most excellent way[11]... And now these three remain, faith, hope and love. But the greatest of these is love.'[12]

Love is the means by which all that is different is held together, because love, more than hope and faith, has an

---

outward dynamic. The systems approach to seeing and under-standing the world is a practical expression of love, because the systems perspective refuses to isolate one thing, or group, or individual, but appreciates the interconnectedness of life, acknowledging that everything interacts with and impacts on the things around it.

A systems approach recognises the interwoven nature of all aspects of life, so the grief or pain felt in one part, or by one party, is both perceptibly and imperceptibly felt by all. The essential story of our world is that of connectedness, and systems thinking maintains this recognition and endeavours to respect the intricate interrelationship and mysterious connec-tions between events, people and the creation itself. Systems thinking acknowledges our interdependence. Things, events, people cannot be understood in isolation, because things, or parts, function the way they do because of other parts. It is not too great a leap of the imagination to suggest that the dynamic that holds these things together in such intricate interrela-tionship is love.[13]

The potential for a clash between the generations is real, and this has to be a cause for concern, because if blaming wins the day, although it may result in action, such action will not fix the problem. For the media, the temptation is to host programmes where the protagonists, young versus old, go at it full pelt. The issue of intergenerational fairness is one of the few that resonates across all age groups: the combination of that universal appeal with furious indignation and pertinent illustrations results in a television or radio producer's dream. For comment writers, intergenerational fairness is likely to be equally irresistible, as anecdote and insult and tart remarks jump off the page for the reader. The risk is that thinking and reflection will be short-circuited, blame will be assigned and relationships across the generations soured, undermining the distinctive accomplishment of the species (see Chapter Five) that enables young people to flourish under the influence of their grandparents' generation.

A pivotal movement?

The argument has been won. We know that the younger generations are angry at their bleak prospects. We also know that in comparison with older generations the cry of 'It's not fair!' is bound to be heard. We also know that this is an issue that is almost global in its extent. The baby boom generation and those a decade older have had wonderful opportunities open up during their lives, and the opportunities available to younger generations seem tawdry in comparison. The prosecution has proved its case. But so what? The challenge rests not in the analysis but in devising and sustaining a response. The tragedy will be if, paralleling the response to environmental concerns, we will be showered with analysis, but the action that follows is slow and uneven.

In response to this exceptional turn of events there are some who will want to express special concern, Christians in particular, but it is not just Christians who carry such a moral concern; there are plenty of people with little or no faith who likewise are concerned to ensure that those of us who are fifty plus do not leave the world a less agreeable place than we found it. The creation of a pivotal movement that seeks ways to *bring the future into the reckoning of today* begins with an invitation to those who have lived lives with opportunities aplenty and in the midst of bountiful public policy, to turn around and practise concern for the future. The challenge as ever will be to the imagination – *what* to do as much as how to do it.

One of the first tasks will be to give politicians confidence that any efforts they make to take future, the 'yet to be born' generations, into account in their policies will not necessarily be rejected at the ballot box. To achieve this might mean petitions, tweets, conventions, debates, leafleting and so on – the sorts of things with which baby boomers are very familiar. With some relish I look forward to reconnecting with the merriment that accompanied the commitment to be a 'woman for peace'. The battle to enable the *rights of the future* to be valued alongside the *rights of today* would bring a greater sense of purpose in life than booking a place on a cruise and boring friends to tears with photographs of 'Elizabeth and I sitting at the Captain's table'. So can we join up in the venture and together work out what needs to happen next? Can we join up to rescue the democratic process from short-termism?

A theological coda

This book has been written from a Christian perspective; however I hope that it will also have proved a helpful read for those who would not claim to have a particular faith. In trying to address both parties I risk having disappointed – or infuriated, both. For Christians – what has been offered may be thought of as Bible-lite and too casual from the perspective of systematic theology. For those who are sceptical about the Christian faith and church practice, then I hope what has been offered has been sufficiently enfolded with humility to temper any rise in blood pressure.

I have taken these risks because of two essential characteristics of the Christian faith that are deeply pertinent to this vexed question of intergenerational fairness. The first is the recognition of this wearisome and mysterious dynamic of sin. You will note that throughout I have replaced this three letter word with a word with three syllables. I have done this, because *dastardly* is a word that stops us in our tracks. We cannot talk about fairness and unfairness, or justice and injustice, unless we are prepared to factor in this recurring dynamic that is energized by our self-interest, but is also a lot more than just this.

Following Jesus in the way in which he lived his life has been offered as a way of acknowledging dastardliness, both by lessening our dastardly behaviour, and redeeming us from the inevitable dastardliness to which we will fall prey. The Church has also been offered as a partial remedy to dastardliness, even though it has little to be proud of in terms of past performance. But what it has achieved are spiritual practices and insights that help to bring out the best in us in our struggle to leave the world a better place than we found it.

The second insight that has been offered from Christian theology is in relation to this issue of scapegoating. When unfairness is so palpable it is an immense temptation to look for a person or a group to blame. A strong case should be made that, along with compassion and commitment to the well-being of others, Christians are to be characterized by their resistance to giving way to blaming. The issue of intergenerational fairness will explode in our faces unless Christians take this gift of Jesus' life and teaching more seriously, and can find ways of sharing this gift with others.

In encouraging people, both Christian and non-Christian alike, to give theology a second chance, my aim is that a resilient theology emerges, that enables us to insist that hopelessness and passivity are not the final words. Resilient theology enables us to see new possibilities and garner the intentionality to practise these possibilities. But even more than this, resilient theology continually acknowledges human frailty to the extent that perfection is never expected. Otherwise the wonderful, liberating generosity of being treated better than we deserve – this ultimate 'alternative performance' that Jesus offers – becomes unnecessary. And what does this mean in relation to our efforts to be a pivotal movement that endeavours to put the future in the same frame as today? It means that our actions only have to be *good enough* because of our confidence 'That all shall be well and all manner of things shall be well',[14] because of the love of God enfolding all Creation.

Notes

1. S. de Beauvoir (1972) *The Coming of Age,* Trans. P. O'Brian, New York: G P Putnam's Sons p.4,5.
2. This is the opening paragraph of Simone de Beauvoir's groundbreaking text on old age, *The Coming of Age,* ibid. p.1.
3. Given the subject in hand – the perceived advantage that has accrued to the baby boom generation – the focus is on younger generations who are at risk of falling prey to resentment. However, resentment affects all ages; older people are not spared the sentiment.
4. The mysterious nature of this interrelationship prompted the popular image of the movement of a butterfly's wings in one continent having an influence on the weather in another.
5. For more on systemic thinking see P. M. Senge (1990) *The Fifth Discipline: The Art and Practice of the Learning Organization,* New York: Doubleday or visit *www.infed.org.* There is also an extensive section on systems thinking in my book *Bothered and Bewildered: Enacting Hope in Troubled Times,* (2009) London: Continuum pp. 49–54.
6. J. Gough, 'The sacred mystery of capitalism', *Prospect* July 2008, p.40.
7. G. Allport (1954) *The Nature of Prejudice,* Reading MA: Addison-Wesley.
8. See R. Girard (1977) *Violence and the Sacred,* trans by P. Gregory; Baltimore: Johns Hopkins University Press and R. Girard (1986) *The Scapegoat,* Baltimore: Johns Hopkins University Press.

211

9. Walter Wink in his *Powers* trilogy likewise rejoices in the capacity of the Gospels, and particularly the actions and teaching of Jesus, to unmask scapegoating, oppression and death dealing. See Walter Wink's *Powers Trilogy*: (1984) *Naming the Powers: The Language of Power in the New Testament*, Philadelphia: Fortress Press; (1986) *Unmasking the Powers: The Invisible Forces That Determine Human Existence*, Philadelphia: Fortress Press; and (1992) *Engaging the Powers: Discernment and Resistance in a World of Domination*, Minneapolis: Fortress Press. In *The Powers That Be: Theology for a New Millennium* (1999), New York: Doubleday, Wink unites his thinking in a single volume.

10. 1 Cor. 12:20 NIV.

11. 1 Cor. 12:31 NIV.

12. 1 Cor. 13:13 NIV.

13. A. Morisy (2009) *Bothered and Bewildered: Enacting Hope in Troubled Times*, London: Continuum p. 50.

14. This lovely phrase is ascribed to Mother Julian of Norwich.

Questions for Discussion

Chapter One: Uniquely favoured? Uniquely selfish? Uniquely fearful?

1. What do you think of the adage 'People resemble their times more than they resemble their parents?'

   As a baby boomer I suggest that the times that shaped me were characterized by optimism and more than a hint of superiority. How would you describe the characteristics of the times that shaped you?

2. 'For the untested generation of non-poor baby boomers, this change in the economic climate not just shocks, but forces us into the uncharted terrain of uncertainty, no longer knowing what to do for the best, and facing the challenge of achieving a previously unknown degree of resilience.'

   Is the baby boom generation as untested as I suggest? What would resilience look like in the context of austerity? Where do you see resilience in action?

3. Is it appropriate for older people, soon to be drawing down their diminished private pensions, to express indignation and to protest, given that they (we) are the generation who, prior to this, has been treated exceptionally fairly and has been exceptionally lucky?

Chapter Two: What's the score?

1. Some factors that offset the increasing dependency ratio between workers and dependents are described in this chapter:
   - there are likely to be fewer dependent children
   - an increase in women in the workforce
   - fewer days lost through sickness and industrial disputes
   - older people retain their capacities for longer
   - social innovation based on ingenuity and good institutions.

   To what extent are you convinced by such mitigating factors?
2. How do you account for the low birth rate in most 'advanced' nations?
3. In your discussions, consider the extent to which 'blame' gets apportioned? Does blaming achieve anything?

Chapter Three: Borrowing from the future

1. Do you think that for middle-aged and younger generations 'the joys of life seem shop soiled and stale'? I suggest that one of the reasons why the shine has gone from life for younger generations is because they are worried about the future, but I am not convinced about this; there may be other factors that play a part. What do you think?
2. Older people as a majority group in relation to our democratic processes have a strong impact on politicians and the decisions they make. Is it appropriate to counter this? And if so, how could this be done?
3. How realistic do you think it is that people might opt to vote on the basis of a concern for the long term?

Chapter Four: Second chance theology

1. Wilkinson and Pickett's research suggests the species Homo sapiens is vulnerable to having too many good things. What do you think? They make the case that as nations get richer and richer, a point is reached when increases in wellbeing and health begin to stall, and levels of anxiety and depression start to gain momentum. Does this fit with your perception and your experience?

2. Traditionally, religions have provided people with the motivation to control desire and unruly emotions and passions. Do you consider religion has the capacity to do this again, without bullying people to behave in certain ways, or by making people feel pathologically guilty?

3. I suggest that although religions often claim and are perceived to be dealing in absolutes, religion is inevitably shaped by the wider culture in which it exists. This means that the emphasis which religion takes at a particular time and place is, in part, informed by the culture of the era. What do you think?

4. Jesus says that 'The man who would save his life will lose it and the person who gives up his life for the sake of others will find his life.' This insight is endorsed by researchers in the field of positive psychology. Do you also endorse this view?

Chapter Five: Age has its purpose?

1. I suggest that we experience a distance between our 'inside' age and the age we see ourselves to be when we look in the mirror, and to which others respond. Does this fit with your experience? If it does, how old do you feel yourself to

be deep inside? And what sort of effect does this have on you?

2. What do you think about the different styles of thinking that cognitive psychologists have identified? Does this fit with your experience? Do you have any illustrations you can share?

3. The chapter concludes by proposing that there are special and important tasks to take on in the third age, for example the stewardship of the culture and the development of spiritual capital. How equipped do you feel older people are for such tasks? What opportunities are there to deliver on the distinctive aptitudes associated with the third age?

Chapter Six: Retirement matters

1. This chapter introduces two important ideas:
   - that increasing the retirement age is not the best way of easing the pressure on younger generations
   - that we need the commitment of an older generation to be a 'pivot' generation, willing to embrace the task of turning the pattern of advantage towards younger and future generations.

   How do you react to these ideas?

2. To be able to contemplate the possibility of acting as part of a 'pivot' generation, confidence is needed in the notion that we need far less income than we realize to live a fulfilled life. Where do you stand in relation to this?

3. What ways can you think of that would help to 'pivot' and turn the direction of advantage towards younger and future generations?

Chapter Seven: Inheritance matters

1. Our wealth, especially the wealth represented in house ownership, is primarily for my children to inherit.
   or:
   Our wealth, especially the wealth represented in house ownership, is primarily to meet the cost of my future care. Which of these is it to be?
   N.B. The opinions of those with no assets, and those with so many assets they can meet both possibilities, are equally valid as the opinions of those for whom this is an active dilemma.
2. I suggest that the stress and strain of meeting the everyday tasks at the heart of family life may have become so onerous that a tipping point has been reached, making the precariousness of the single or unattached life preferable to the hard work and emotional intensity of family life. What do you think?
3. How do you rate friendship in your life? Could you see the possibility of friendship networks providing the support that is usually seen as the responsibility of the immediate family, especially in relation to the care of those in deep old age?

Chapter Eight: An epidemic of narcissism?

1. Do you consider that in our society healthy self-regard has toppled over into problematic narcissism? In what ways is narcissism problematic?
2. I make the case that in an individualistic society where social rules are easily ignored, the idea of sin becomes irrelevant, and I suggest that rather than think in terms of sin we should use the idea of struggle, and the avoidance of struggle, as the worst state into which we can fall. What do you think about this?

3. Is there any hope for Homo sapiens? If there is hope, how do we best act on it?

Chapter Nine: Pivot: Paying our proper dues

1. Inheritance tax.... What do you think about it?
2. To what extent do you feel we have to take responsibility for our loneliness? I suggest that when we are pained by loneliness it can be hard to resist lashing out verbally at those who make an effort to come close. Does this ring true from your experience?
3. I conclude this chapter with strong rhetoric, 'If we are to embrace Erikson's challenge of "grand generativity" then we owe it to younger and future generations to expose bogus routes to wellbeing, and we have to articulate this by our actions and habits as well as through our wise words.' What actions would ground or root this sentiment?

Chapter Ten: Old people ... don't make me laugh

1. It was around 1985 when Wolfensberger suggested that society had 'deep-seated destructive intentions'. With an abortion rate running at one in five of all pregnancies in the UK, environmental degradation causing massive destruction and loss of life through landslides and flooding, as well as a call for 'aid-in-dying', was Wolfensberger a needless scaremonger or a prophet we should heed?
2. What do you think of the idea of 'bizarre returns of repressed behaviour'? I cite some forms of humour and the extent to which death has become entertainment as examples of such bizarre returns. How do you make sense of death as entertainment?

3. Florida Scott Maxwell, reflecting on her experience of deep old age writes:

> 'We wonder how much older we have to become, and what degree of decay we may have to endure. We keep whispering to ourselves, "Is this age yet? How much further must I go?" For age can be dreaded more than death...It is waiting for death that wears us down, and the distaste for what we may become.'[1]

There is a fearful honesty in her observation. How does her description fit with your perception of the journey into 'deep' old age?

Chapter Eleven: Resentment: The dastardly bushfire

1. 'For each of us, our situation a few decades on will be the same as that which is allotted to the old today.' Consider this aphorism; to what extent do you agree?
2. What are your thoughts on the way the media, whether television, radio or the papers, handle the issue of inter-generational fairness? And electronic media: the Web, Facebook and so on, what about their role?
3. Do you believe it is realistic to think that older generations, and the baby boom generation in particular, would be willing to be a 'pivot' generation, willing to work to bring the 'future' into political considerations, even though this would mean voting for polices that were not in one's own immediate interest?

Note

1. F. Scott Maxwell (1968) *The Measure of my Days*, New York: Alfred A. Knopf p. 138.

Index